A moment's monument

The House of Life

THE SONNET

A sonnet is a moment's monument,—
  Memorial from the Soul's eternity
  To one dead deathless hour. Look that it be,
Whether for lustral rite or dire portent,
Of its own arduous fulness reverent:
  Carve it in ivory or in ebony,
  As Day or Night may rule; and let Time see
Its flowering crest impearled and orient.

A Sonnet is a coin: its face reveals
  The soul,—its converse, to what Power 't is due:—
Whether for tribute to the august appeals
  Of Life, or dower in Love's high retinue,
It serve; or, 'mid the dark wharf's cavernous breath,
In Charon's palm it pay the toll to Death.
          [1880]   [1881]

D. G. Rossetti

A moment's monument

The development of the sonnet

Gertrude M. White
Joan G. Rosen

CHARLES SCRIBNER'S SONS   NEW YORK

*To Robert G. Hoopes,
our colleague and friend,
who suggested this book*

ACKNOWLEDGMENTS

Grateful acknowledgment is made to the following authors, publishers, agents, and individuals for their permission to reprint the poems in this anthology:

MARGARET AVISON. For "Butterfly Bones or Sonnet Against Sonnets."

DONALD BABCOCK. For "America."

THE BODLEY HEAD. For rights in Canada for Roy Campbell, "Familiar Daemon."

CHATTO AND WINDUS LTD. For rights in Canada for Wilfred Owen, "Anthem for Doomed Youth" and "The End" from *The Collected Poems of Wilfred Owen.*

THOMAS Y. CROWELL. For Leonie Adams, "Thought's End" from *Poems: A Selection,* Copyright 1954 by Leonie Adams.

CURTIS BROWN, LTD. For rights in Canada for Roy Campbell, "The Serf."

For Donald Hall, "The Funeral" from *The Dark Houses.*

THE JOHN DAY COMPANY, INC. For John Manifold, "The Sirens." Copyright 1946 by The John Day Company, reprinted from *Selected Verse*

DODD, MEAD & COMPANY, INC. For rights in the United States for Rupert Brooke, "A Channel Passage" and "The Soldier."

GERALD DUCKWORTH. For Charlotte Mew, "Not for That City" from *Collected Poems,* 1952.

NORMA MILLAY ELLIS. For Edna St. Vincent Millay, "I shall forget you presently, my dear," "On Hearing a Symphony of Beethoven," and "See where Capella with her golden kids" from *Collected Poems,* Harper & Row. Copyright 1921, 1922, 1923, 1928, 1931, 1934, 1948, 1950, 1951, 1955, 1958, 1962, by Edna St. Vincent Millay and Norma Millay Ellis.

FABER AND FABER LTD. For rights in Canada for W. H. Auden, "A Voyage III" ("The Sphinx"), "Our Bias," "Sonnet from China XII," "The Novelist from *Collected Shorter Poems 1927–1957.*

For rights in Canada for two lines quoted from T. S. Eliot, "The Hollow Men" from *Collected Poems 1909–1962.*

For rights in Canada to Stephen Spender, "Daybreak" from *Collected Poems.*

FARRAR, STRAUS & GIROUX, INC. For John Berryman, "NOT TO LIVE: Jamestown, 1957." Reprinted with the permission of Farrar, Straus & Giroux, Inc. Published in the *Virginia Quarterly,* copyright © 1957 by Kate Berryman.

For Robert Lowell, "Words for Hart Crane" from *Life Studies,* copyright 1953 by Robert Lowell.

HARCOURT BRACE JOVANOVICH, INC. For E. E. Cummings, "the Cambridge ladies who live in furnished souls," copyright, 1923, 1951, by E. E. Cummings. Reprinted from his volume, *Poems 1923–1954;* "i like my body when it is with your," copyright, 1925, by E. E. Cummings. Reprinted from his volume, *Poems 1923–1954;* "this is the garden: colours come and go," copyright, 1925, 1953, by E. E. Cummings. Reprinted from his volume, *Poems 1923–1954;* "pity this busy monster, manunkind," copyright, 1944, by E. E. Cummings. Reprinted from his volume, *Poems 1923–1954;* "honour corruption villainy holiness," copyright, 1950, by E. E. Cummings. Reprinted from his volume, *Poems 1923–1954;* "serene immediate silliest and whose," copyright, 1931, 1959, by E. E. Cummings. Reprinted from his volume, *Poems 1923–1954.*

For rights in the United States for two lines quoted from T. S. Eliot "The Hollow Men" from *Collected Poems 1909–1962.*

For Robert Lowell, "Concord" from *Lord Weary's Castle,* copyright, 1944, 1946, by Robert Lowell.

DAVID HIGHAM ASSOCIATES, LTD. For Elizabeth Jennings, "Lazarus," from *Song for a Birth or a Death.*

HOLT, RINEHART AND WINSTON, INC. For Robert Frost, "Acquainted with the Night," "Design," "Once by the Pacific," "The Oven Bird," "The Silken Tent," "Putting in the Seed" from *The Poetry of Robert Frost* edited by Edward Connery Lathem. Copyright 1916, 1928, © 1969 by Holt, Rinehart and Winston, Inc. Copyright 1936, 1942, 1944, © 1956 by Robert Frost. Copyright © 1964, 1970 by Lesley Frost Ballantine.

For Winifred Welles, "Cruciform" from *The Shape of Memory.* Copyright 1944 by Holt, Rinehart and Winston, Inc.

HOPE LERESCHE & STEELE. For Christopher Hassall, "Crisis XXVII."

HOUGHTON MIFFLIN COMPANY. For Archibald MacLeish, "The End of the World" from *Collected Poems 1917–1952.*

ALFRED A. KNOPF, INC. For John Crowe Ransom, "Piazza Piece" from *Selected Poems,* 3rd edition. Copyright 1927 and renewed 1955 by John Crowe Ransom. For "The Tall Girl" from *Selected Poems,* 3rd edition. Copyright 1924 and renewed 1952 by John Crowe Ransom.

For Rex Warner, "Mallard" from *Poems.* Copyright 1938 by Alfred A. Knopf, Inc.

LITTLE, BROWN AND COMPANY. For Stanley Kunitz, "Organic Bloom" from *Selected Poems 1928–1958* by Stanley Kunitz. Copyright 1956 by Stanley Kunitz.

LIVERIGHT PUBLISHING CORPORATION. For E. E. Cummings, "next to of course god america i," "if i have made,my lady,intricate" from *Is 5*. Copyright renewed 1953 by Edward Estein Cummings.

THE MACMILLAN COMPANY. For rights in the United States for Thomas Hardy, "At a Lunar Eclipse," "At The Altar Rail," "Hap," "In the Cemetery," "She, to Him," "The Pity of It," and "Zermatt" from *Collected Poems.* Copyright 1925 by The Macmillan Company.

For John Masefield, "Flesh, I have knocked at many a dusty door" and "Here in the self is all that man can know" from *Good Friday and Other Poems.* Copyright 1916 by John Masefield, renewed 1944 by John Masefield.

For Edwin Arlington Robinson, "Many Are Called" from *Collected Poems.* Copyright 1921 by Edwin Arlington Robinson, renewed 1949 by Ruth Nivison. For "New England" and "The Sheaves" from *Collected Poems.* Copyright 1925 by Edwin Arlington Robinson, renewed 1953 by Ruth Nivison and Barbara R. Holt.

For rights in the United States for William Butler Yeats, "Leda And The Swan" from *Collected Poems.* Copyright 1928 by The Macmillan Company, renewed 1956 by Georgie Yeats.

THE MACMILLAN COMPANY OF CANADA LIMITED. For rights in Canada for Thomas Hardy, "At a Lunar Eclipse," "At the Altar Rail," "Hap," "In the Cemetery," "She, to Him," "The Pity of It," and "Zermatt" from *Collected Poems.* Reprinted by permission of the Hardy Estate; Macmillan London & Basingstoke.

McCLELLAND AND STEWARD LIMITED. For rights in Canada for Rupert Brooke, "A Channel Passage" and "The Soldier" from *Collected Poems.*

ANN LESLIE MOORE. For Merrill Moore, "How She Resolved to Act." Copyright in name of Ann Leslie Moore.

NEW DIRECTIONS. For rights in the United States for Wilfred Owen, "Anthem for Doomed Youth" and "The End" from *Collected Poems.* Copyright Chatto & Windus, Ltd. 1946, © 1963.

For Ezra Pound, "A Virginal" from *Personae.* Copyright 1926 by Ezra Pound.

For rights in the United States for Dylan Thomas "Dawn Raid" and "On the Marriage of a Virgin" from *Collected Poems.* Copyright 1943 by New Directions Publishing Corporation.

OXFORD UNIVERSITY PRESS, INC. For Conrad Aiken, "Green, green, and green again, and greener still" and "Shape has no shape, nor will your thinking shape it" from *Collected Poems.* Copyright 1953 by Conrad Aiken.

A. D. PETERS & CO. For Edmund Blunden, "Vlamertinghe: Passing the Chateau, 1917."

For Hilaire Belloc, "We will not whisper, we have found the place."

RANDOM HOUSE, INC. For rights in the United States for W. H. Auden "A Voyage III" ("The Sphinx"), "Our Bias," "Sonnets From China XII," ("In Time of War XVI"), and "The Novelist" from *Collected Shorter Poems 1927–1957*. Copyright © 1966 by W. H. Auden.

For Robinson Jeffers, "Cruel Falcon" and "Love the Wild Swan" from *Selected Poetry of Robinson Jeffers*. Copyright 1935 and renewed 1963 by Donnan Jeffers and Garth Jeffers.

For rights in the United States for Stephen Spender "Daybreak" from *Selected Poems*. Copyright 1942 by Stephen Spender.

HENRY REGNERY COMPANY. For rights in the United States to Roy Campbell, "Familiar Daemon," and "The Serf" from *Selected Poetry*.

CHARLES SCRIBNER'S SONS. For Edwin Arlington Robinson, "Aaron Stark," "Calvary," "Oh, for a Poet," "The Clerks," and "Verlaine" from *The Children of the Night* (1897).

For George Santayana, "Deem not, because you see me in the press," "I would I might forget that I am I," and "Oh world, thou choosest not the better part" from *Poems*. Copyright 1923 Charles Scribner's Sons; renewal copyright 1951.

For Allen Tate, "Sonnet at Christmas—No. 2" from *Poems*. Copyright 1931, 1932, 1937, 1948 by Charles Scribner's Sons; renewal copyright © 1959, 1960 by Allen Tate.

SIDGWICK & JACKSON LTD. For John Gawsworth, "Edward Thomas" from *Collected Poems*.

THE SWALLOW PRESS, INC. For Yvor Winters, "To Emily Dickinson" from *Collected Poems* © 1960.

A. P. WATT & SON. For rights in Canada to W. B. Yeats "Leda and the Swan" from *The Collected Poems of W. B. Yeats*, by permission of Mrs. W. B. Yeats and the Macmillan Company of Canada.

Contents

Sir Philip Sidney

Henry Constable

Samuel Daniel

Michael Drayton

Giles Fletcher

Joshua Sylvester

Fulke Greville, Baron Brooke

Barnabe Barnes

William Drummond of Hawthornden

William Shakespeare

John Donne

George Herbert

John Milton

❧ The Eighteenth Century   62

Thomas Gray

William Cowper

Anna Seward

❧ The Romantic Period   66

William Wordsworth

Blanco White

James Leigh Hunt

The Nineteenth Century   92

Richard Chevenix Trench

Charles Tennyson-Turner

Henry Wadsworth Longfellow

Edgar Allan Poe

Westland Marston

Matthew Arnold

George Meredith

Dante Gabriel Rossetti

Edwin Arlington Robinson

Hilaire Belloc

Robert Frost

John Masefield

Donald C. Babcock

Ezra Pound

Rupert Brooke

Robinson Jeffers

Introduction

More than four hundred years ago two cultivated Englishmen found a particular pattern of the short poem in Italy and brought it home with them. Since then the sonnet has shown itself to be the hardiest and most versatile of English lyric forms. Beginning as the poem of a medieval literary convention, that of courtly love, it has adapted to changes in subject matter, tone, language, and structure, while recognizably retaining its own character. It is the purpose of this anthology to present a selection of the finest sonnets written in English from the middle of the sixteenth century to our own day and thereby to demonstrate the seemingly inexhaustible capacity of this brief form to express the thoughts and feelings of different men in different times.

In bygone years it was easy enough to define a sonnet and to lay down hard and fast criteria for sonnet excellence. Particularly during the nineteenth century, when the sonnet was again flourishing after a period of neglect, many critics occupied themselves with attempts at such poetic legislation. Meanwhile, poets went on writing sonnets to please themselves. And while many sonnets continued to be conventional enough in form to satisfy the most exacting judge, others as good or better made the rules look foolish. This is particularly true of sonnets written in the last fifty years.

What, then, is a sonnet? The word itself comes from the diminutive of the Italian *suono*, "sound": *sonnetto*, "a little sound." As this implies, the term originally meant any of a variety of short poems accompanied by music; there were at first no fixed requirements for length or for rhyme pattern. The first "legitimate" sonnet was composed by Fra Guittone d'Arezzo in the middle of the thirteenth century in the form now familiar as the "Italian" sonnet. Its two parts, octave and sestet, are sharply separated by their rhyme scheme, the octave rhyming *a b b a a b b a,* the sestet usually either in two tercets, *c d e c d e,* or in six alternately rhymed lines, *c d c d c d.* The Italian poets were never, however, the purists some English and American critics of a later day supposed; and variations, especially in the rhymes of the sestet, were common.

No sooner had the sonnet reached England than English poets were combining the traditional octave with a sestet ending in a couplet, thereby creating a hybrid form. Whatever subsequent critics have declared, this form has been employed for some of the most famous and successful sonnets written in English. Meanwhile, an "English" form of the sonnet had been invented, avoiding the octave/ sestet division and consisting instead of three quatrains and a couplet: *a b a b c d c d e f e f g g*. Edmund Spenser, the great Elizabethan poet, invented and gave his name to the Spenserian variation of the English sonnet, using linked rhymes in its quatrains: *a b a b b c b c c d c d e e*. All forms, whatever their variations in rhyme scheme, had in common the decasyllabic iambic line and most—though not all— were fourteen lines in length.

These distinctions seem clear enough. Having differentiated the forms according to their rhyme schemes, the critic can proceed to analyze the diverse effects produced by the "swell and ebb" of the Italian pattern, the "whiplash" of the couplet following the more loosely structured quatrains of the English sonnet, or the harmoni- ously linked melody of the Spenserian form. He may, if of a pedantic turn of mind, complain of the "illegitimacy" of the English form or the irregularity of the rhyme scheme of Shelley's "Ozymandias." But a reading of sonnets will reveal that few poets have felt bound by strict rules and definitions. Rather, they have from the beginning varied basic rhyme schemes with great freedom, even occasionally employing couplets or blank verse instead of the more usual pat- terns. Poems recognizably sonnet-like in effect have extended to fifteen or sixteen lines in length. Even the traditional tyranny of the decasyllabic iambic line has been broken, first by that great innovator Gerard Manley Hopkins and subsequently by many contemporary poets. Now poets use meter, stress, and rhyme in sonnets as they see fit; and irregular forms flourish alongside firmly traditional ones.

The fact is that neither rhyme pattern nor length nor meter, as such, but rather internal principles of intellectual and emotional structure identify the sonnet. Despite its name, the sonnet is not a song. It is dramatic in nature, rather than lyric. Characteristically, it begins with a scene or image drawn from the external world, com- pares it by statement, implication, or symbol with some state of mind or emotion, and through analogy thus reflects upon or presents an insight into some particular or universal situation. Essentially it objectifies an inner conflict of some kind, commenting on or resolving it in brief compass. It is far more logical in structure, more precise in thought, more concise and unified in both substance and design than the ordinary lyric. Its symmetry, its very life, is the internal logic, intellectual and emotional, that governs the balance and relationship of its parts. The qualities of a good sonnet are found not in its conformity to some external pattern but in its unity of design, condensation of thought, exactitude of language and image, and— even at its most meditative and abstract—its essentially dramatic nature.

That the sonnet answers in some way to the movement of the mind, to the nature of intellectual and emotional experience, is demonstrated by its ability to adapt, to extend its range, to accommodate within its brief compass a wide variety of subjects, of attitudes, of effects. From the time of its origin to our own day a host of poets have used and are still using it to express and to dramatize their perceptions. This anthology is a record of and a testimony to the power and beauty of which this form, both traditional and experimental, is capable.

The Renaissance

The origin of the sonnet has been a matter of much speculation and controversy, but the Italian writers of the thirteenth century—whether they derived it from the Greek epigram, the Provençal troubadours, or the court of Frederick II of Sicily—were the first to give it definite, permanent shape and character. Once devised, the form rapidly became popular in Italy and was brought to its perfection by Dante and Petrarch. Dante's *Vita Nuova* and Petrarch's *Canzoniere* furnished the model both in manner and matter for poets throughout Europe.

Of the two, the influence of Petrarch was by far the greater. Dante, for the men of the Renaissance, was associated with the past, with the medieval world. By contrast Petrarch, in his individuality, subjectivity, and curiosity seemed like a modern. It was thus the *Canzoniere* that fixed the form, the content, the themes, and the conceits of European love poetry for generations.

The framework of the story is familiar: the meeting and sudden love; the lady's coldness and repulse of the lover; his devotion, by turns timid, ardent, amorous, idealized, hopeful, despairing; his temporary turning for consolation to another; the lady's death; her forgiveness and intercession for him in heaven; his imagined meeting with her there. Embodying attitudes largely inherited from the Provençal troubadours and their Courts of Love, these sonnets are not so much vehicles of the shadowy story as conscious exercises of intellect and imagination on the all-absorbing subject. They touch on other topics: religious and political feeling, affection for friends of the same sex, sometimes even the sensual aspects of love; in fact, they include many of the subsequent variations of theme treated in the sonnet. But their main aim is the exaltation of an ideal type of beauty and a particular kind of love relationship, in which the lover is led through the worship of physical beauty to the knowledge and love of virtue and eventually to spiritual purification and joy in heaven.

The popularity and influence of Petrarch are difficult to exaggerate. Chaucer's Clerk, toward the end of the fourteenth century, mentions him:

Fraunceys Petrak, the lauriat poete
Highte this clerk, whos rethorike sweete
Enlumyned al Ytaille of poetrie

By the sixteenth century "Petrarchismo"—a term applied to imitations of the poet more artificial than artful—was at its height; and his rhetoric was illuminating, and too often blinding, the poets of France and of England.

II

In England, the history of the sonnet falls into two distinct parts. It is well known that Sir Thomas Wyatt and Henry Howard, Earl of Surrey, divide the honor of introducing it, as a result of their travels and studies in Italy. Their sonnets, first published in 1557 in a collection called *Tottel's Miscellany,* are the earliest examples of the form written in English. But they were not immediately nor widely influential. For a quarter of a century the sonnet lapsed into virtual disuse, to be reintroduced into England mainly from France. Most Elizabethan sonneteers derived their chief knowledge of Petrarch and his Italian followers not from Wyatt and Surrey but from French adaptations by the poets of La Pleiade, particularly Ronsard and Desportes. The true parents of the Elizabethan sonnet, thus, are Thomas Watson, who, in 1582, published *Hecatompathia,* or *The Passionate Century of Love,* a collection of sonnets (so-called, though they were poems of eighteen lines) that were paraphrases and translations of the French imitators of Petrarch; Sir Philip Sidney, whose *Astrophel and Stella,* in 1591, touched off the sonnet sequence craze; and Edmund Spenser, whose *Amoretti,* in 1595, were the truest sequence of the decade.

Sidney, Spenser, and Shakespeare are, of course, the great names among Elizabethan sonneteers. But their very greatness obscures the fact that otherwise there is little really memorable work in the sonnet in this period of great lyric achievement. Of the vast number of sonnets published in England during the sixteenth century, the great majority are mere literary exercises. The early history of the sonnet in England is largely the history of the acclimatization and adaptation of foreign models and foreign conventions to the native accent, a process that began with Sir Thomas Wyatt.

Wyatt's sonnets, it should be borne in mind, are inferior as poetry to his lyrics, some of which are justly famous in an age of fine lyrics. None of his sonnets, in fact, will bear comparison to his "Awake, My Lute," or "Forget Not Yet the Tried Intent." The interest of Wyatt's sonnets is historical. They show a gifted poet struggling to adapt the Italian model to the as yet unsettled state of the English language.

None of Wyatt's thirty-two sonnets strictly follows the Italian rhyme scheme. He follows Petrarch in the octave, but closes the sestet with a rhymed couplet, thereby—according to a learned historian of English poetry—"leading all English sonnet writers before Milton on a wrong path." [1] Certainly the couplet ending alters the whole balance of the Italian sonnet, substituting an epigrammatic, logical ending for the gentle rise and fall of the Petrarchan sonnet. This alteration of the form seems to mirror Wyatt's temperamental and intellectual difference from his model; for where Petrarch's appeal is primarily to the imagination and the heart, Wyatt's is to the mind. In his choice of sonnets to translate, he passes over the more emotional in favor of those in which a conceit is carefully worked out in logical terms. In fact, despite his experiments with versification, Wyatt's main preoccupation is with matter, and his mature concern is to explore the psychological and moral implications of courtly love. His sonnets exhibit a closely reasoned introspection, a logical exploitation of the conceit, and individual energy of thought and feeling. The joint product of form and content is a poem reflecting a view of life directly antithetical to that of Petrarch: rational rather than imaginative, empirical rather than transcendental, independent and self-assertive rather than romantic.

Surrey, Wyatt's younger contemporary, was a more conscious artist, though not so great a poet. His sonnets are marked by more grace and elegance, a more skillful use of accent and caesura, and far less sense of an individual and sturdy mind and spirit. He was the first to write harmonious English verse in the now fully developed language. He ignored the elaborate rhyme scheme of the Italian sonnet and employed instead a new sonnet form that he devised and bequeathed to a greater successor: thus it has come to be known as the "Shakespearean" sonnet form. This pattern consists of three quatrains in alternate rhyme, closing with a couplet. The usual arrangement is *a b a b c d c d e f e f g g,* though here, too, variations of rhyme scheme are possible. Whatever pattern of

---

[1] W. J. Courthope, *A History of English Poetry* (London, 1895–1910), II, 91.

rhyme is employed in the three quatrains, however, the Shake-spearean or English sonnet always closes with a couplet.

III

Wyatt and Surrey both died young; and after its promising be-ginning the sonnet in England languished until the publication of Watson's *Hecatompathia* in 1582. This collection sounded again, and more strongly, what was to be the keynote of all but the greatest of Elizabethan sonnets: they were a summary of all the exaggerated conventions of "Petrarchismo." Petrarch's Italian and French fol-lowers had found it easier to imitate the most artificial aspects of his style—the recurrent images, the exaggerated conceits, the tricks of rhetoric and phrase, the conventional situations and attitudes—than his lofty idealism, his penetration into complex and contradictory psychological states, or his union of subtle thought and deep feeling. In their hands his art became artificial in both form and content. "Petrarchismo is the art of treating cleverly and wittily matters of the heart, of composing love poems without the emotion in the soul, of feigning passion for an imaginary mistress, and of singing a fiction of amorous intrigue, whose phases and whose stages were fixed, and, as it were, established by an immovable tradition." [2] This description applies to most of the sonnets produced in England during the sixteenth century, particularly to those forming part of one of the fashionable sonnet sequences. The Elizabethan sonneteers took over the machinery bequeathed them by Petrarch's imitators. Thousands of sonnets set forth the theme of love; celebrated, pleaded with, and wasted in despair over a lovely but cruel mistress; analyzed the baleful effects of love on the mental and physical state of the lover; lamented absence from the lady; besought the soothing min-istrations of Care-Charmer Sleep; toyed with pretty, ingenious, some-times ridiculous, but always conventional conceits in which com-parisons to the lover's heart, soul, and situation were drawn from natural history, mythology, and the universal experiences of every-day life.

It is necessary to emphasize the artificial, conventional nature of the Elizabethan sonnet, for the question to what extent any of them may be regarded as autobiographical or self-revelatory has been much canvassed. This is particularly true in the cases of Sidney and

[2] J. M. Berdan, *Early Tudor Poetry*, 1485-1547 (New York, 1920), p. 460.

Shakespeare, whose greatness as poets lends them additional interest as men, and whose poems seem to speak in the accents of felt truth. Opinions concerning the autobiographical element in Shakespeare's sonnets range from acceptance of them as a factual record of historical and psychological events, to interpretation of them as an extended metaphor in which the poet is working out in lyric form ideas and themes later developed in his plays.[3] There can be no doubt that fine sonnets of this period, like fine lyric poetry of any period, penetrate into and express genuine, and genuinely experienced, psychic states. They may, indeed, begin in some personal situation or refer to some particular event. But recent investigation has tended to conclude that they should not be regarded as autobiographical or as a medium for personal confession, but may best be understood in the light of the literary conventions they embody.

IV

Sidney's *Astrophel and Stella* showed his generation the dramatic possibilities of the sonnet sequence. Unlike the lesser poets of the time, he employed the Petrarchan conventions with such power as to convey the impression of reality. Although most of his ideas and many of his phrases themselves are derivative, his forceful and individual style—the voice of a personality striking in an age of exceptional men—gives the impression of credible personal emotion. His record of the adventures of the soul of Astrophel under the sway of love still compels assent, as he chronicles the many changes of mood: from gallantry and devotion to desire, from desire to melancholy and revulsion, then to self-disgust and an eventual rejection of earthly love for a clearer knowledge and embrace of spiritual love. Conforming to the Petrarchan rules, exploiting the characteristic themes and metaphors, the whole an exercise on the set subject of the conflict between love and virtue, the sequence still appears a personal and intimate story. "To Sidney's contemporaries, *Astrophel and Stella* seemed a revelation of the poet's soul." [4]

After the publication of *Astrophel and Stella,* most of the poets of

---

[3] For the first view, see J. Dover Wilson, *The Sonnets* (Cambridge, 1966); for the second, see James Winny, *The Master-Mistress: A Study of Shakespeare's Sonnets* (New York, 1968).

[4] J. Erskine, *The Elizabethan Lyric* (New York, 1967), p. 130.

the time produced sonnet sequences, most of which are unreadable today. Lacking Sidney's serious temper and depth of feeling, his contemporaries made use of the sonnet as a mere fashionable exercise. The very names of these sequences—Giles Fletcher's *Licia,* William Percy's *Coelia,* William Smith's *Chloria,* Bartholomew Griffin's *Fidessa*—breathe the air of deserted ballrooms hung with faded paper flowers. Only a rare individual sonnet, like Barnabe Barnes' "Content" or Henry Constable's "My lady's presence makes the roses red," survive to remind us of a vanished host of poems.

Perhaps the best of the sequences by lesser Elizabethan poets are Samuel Daniel's *Delia* and Michael Drayton's *Idea's Mirror. Delia* is as lyric as *Astrophel and Stella* is dramatic. Daniel, whose purity of diction was much praised in his own day and later, attempted with some success to use the themes and devices of the Italian and French sonneteers as gracefully in English as had they in their native tongues. His sonnets exhibit the first extended use of the Shakespearean form, and both in their structure and in his use of the "eternizing" theme—the power of verse to make love immortal against time and barbarism—prepared the way, more than those of any other contemporary, for the sonnets of Shakespeare. Drayton's sequence, by contrast, harks back to Sidney in its changes of mood, its dramatic energy and colloquial language, its particularization of event and undercurrent of honesty, and at least once reaches the very heights in the famous "Since there's no help, come, let us kiss and part."

But it was Edmund Spenser, "prince of poets in his time," whose *Amoretti* are at once the truest sequence and, in their transcendental idealism, the most genuinely Petrarchan of all Elizabethan sonnets. In their story of pure love attained, however, they turn from the romance theme of courtly love to the celebration of virtuous courtship. Rather than the conflict of flesh and spirit, Spenser portrays their reconciliation. Along with this shift in theme, the emphasis moves from the psychological state of the lover to the beauty and virtues of the lady. Her physical beauty, though described in detail, is the embodiment and reflection of her spiritual beauty; and worship of her leads the lover not to rejection of earthly love and subsequent reunion in heaven, but through love of the body to the spirit and joy both here and hereafter.

Spenser solved the problem of adequate structure, the lack of which is the notable weakness of most sequences, by his device of linking individual sonnets to the changing seasons of the year. Each sonnet, though separate in itself, takes its appointed place in a measured progression, the sedate inner drama paced and paralleled by the slow and stately rhythms of nature. The sense of a harmonious wholeness is reinforced by the poet's placid tone, his reflective mood, and his musical and fluid style, and enhanced also by his rhyme scheme, which differs from both the Italian and the English pattern. Spenser's sonnets are rhymed *a b a b b c b c c d c d e e,* thus avoiding both the division of octave and sestet and the sharply distinguished progression of rhymes that characterize, respectively, the Petrarchan and the Shakespearean forms. Instead, the repetition of rhyme binds the whole more closely together and harmonizes the separate sonnets into a total composition. Though no one sonnet, perhaps, reaches those heights that Shakespeare, Sidney, and others occasionally attained, the sequence as a whole makes an effect inferior only to that masterpiece, the *Epithalamion.*

If the Amoretti are the crown of Elizabethan sonnet sequences, Shakespeare's sonnets, like his plays, are the delight and wonder of his age or any age. Far too much energy has been invested, far too much ink spilled in arguments over the identity of the Friend and the Dark Lady, in attempts to piece together the personal story that some believe they tell, or in analyses of the psychological states and the nature of the relationships they may depict. Shakespeare's sonnets exist not as history nor as biography nor yet as true confessions, but as poetry. And like all poetry, they exist by virtue of their imaginative power, depth of feeling, energy and justness of metaphor, command of language. They are the voice of imagination, penetrating and illuminating human experience. Because they are great poems they suffer from too much concern with the possible biographical relations between the poet and his poetry.

As do other Elizabethan sonnets, Shakespeare's poems exhibit a recurrent use of the themes and conventions of Petrarchan love poetry. Like Spenser, he attempted to solve the problem of sensual versus spiritual love. Unlike Spenser, he reached out beyond love itself to seek his central theme in the antinomies of human experience, the predicament of man in a universe where beauty coexists with corruption, truth with mutability, and all is ruled by the universal tyranny of Time. His praise of beauty always emphasizes the approach of decay, and his sonnets give the "eternizing" theme its most powerful and persistent statement. Love, which for other poets is a personal experience, a means of individual joy, sorrow, or salvation, in these sonnets becomes—along with the art that immortalizes it—the answer to that cosmic flux that beats forever upon the high shores of the world. The unique value of Shakespeare's sonnets lies not in the biographical problems they present but in their rich and complex texture, their combination of intellectual precision, metaphorical power, and intense feeling, the wide vistas they open into the life of man, beleaguered incessantly by the contradictions of his own spirit and the cruelties and complexities of the universe.

V

By the end of the century and the death of Elizabeth in 1603, the fashion of the Petrarchan love sonnet had burnt itself out. The conditions, social and cultural, that had produced and encouraged it had changed, and a new age had begun for England and for poetry. The Petrarchan idealization of love had bred its own antidote, the mocking, independent note of defiance and rejection of love's tyranny that had sounded ever and anon since Wyatt's "A Renouncing of Love." The extraordinary popularity of the Petrarchan school had, in the first place, been due to conditions and influences no longer viable. Humanism, which had spread the idea of Platonic love, had given way to an increased Puritanism and the growth of a critical attitude toward love, and particularly the excesses of the courtly love code, as immoral or trivial. The Tudor nobles had sought to unite themselves with the past and had looked toward Italy as the home of ancient tradition and contemporary learning and culture. The Puritan middle classes, the trade war with Italy, and the rise of dissension between Crown and Parliament meant a new and Philistine insularity. Revulsion against Italy and things Italian fed on religious bigotry, fear of the Inquisition and of political plots, and a tendency already evident in the Tudor age to associate the homeland of Dante and Petrarch with all manner of vice and immorality. All these circumstances, together with the weariness and impatience generated by floods of inferior sonnets by inferior poets, helped to bring about the decline of the Petrarchan fashion. But in the hands of a great poet, John Donne, the sonnet form itself was to give striking proof of its ability to adapt and transform itself to changing conditions and changing themes.

The use of the Petrarchan sonnet for themes other than romantic love was by no means an innovation. Petrarch himself, like Dante before him, had used the sonnet to express religious feeling. In England, the reaction against Petrarchan convention already mentioned had manifested itself from the beginning both in an independent treatment of traditional themes and in the appearance of sonnets on religious subjects. In 1591, the same year *Astrophel and Stella* first appeared, Henry Constable published a sonnet series called *Spiritual Sonnets to the Honour of God and Hys Saintes.* Barnabe Barnes's *A Divine Centurie of Spirituall Sonnets* appeared in 1595. Sidney's "Leave me, O love . . ." and Spenser's "Easter" are among the finest sonnets of the age. But the great bulk of Elizabethan sonnets "wore Venus' livery" as George Herbert complained; and whatever its departures from "Petrarchismo" in the hands of genius, the sonnet had failed to evolve a new central theme that could replace courtly love.

VI

Donne's "Holy Sonnets" announce a new chapter in the history of the sonnet. Until those of Gerard Manley Hopkins, whose poetry, written in the nineteenth century, was not published until 1918, they remained the greatest sonnets written in English on religious subjects. The best of them are incomparable in their union of those diverse qualities that characterize "metaphysical" poetry and that, through Donne and his followers, introduced new modes of thought and feeling into lyric poetry.

Donne's sonnets, like his earlier love lyrics and his epigrams and satires, reject most of the poetical furniture of the time: the courtly love tradition, the poetic diction of archaic or euphonious words so dear to Spenser, the classical story and allusion, the descriptive epithet drawn from nature, and any interest in plot or sense of the dramatic relation of man to man. In place of these they employ a muscular vocabulary, a varied and colloquial diction, a direct, harsh, abrupt versification, a new use of the old sonnet conceits and a new metaphor drawn from science and divinity. Never conventional and never interested in generalization, the "Holy Sonnets" depict an inner drama of heart and soul in which all the resources of a subtle and witty mind are placed at the service of fervent feeling. They are intense, tormented, and as personal as Donne's earlier love poetry when, as a young man, he had addressed a mistress rather than God.

VII

By and large, by the early seventeenth century the first great period of sonnet writing was over. Except for George Herbert, Donne's younger contemporary and follower, who wrote a few sonnets, the seventeenth-century poets, from Ben Jonson to Abraham Cowley, turned to other models and to other influences. It remained for the greatest of them, John Milton, to revive the sonnet, revise its form, change and diversify its content, and impress it for two hundred years with the stamp of his personality and his genius.

It is easier to characterize Milton's sonnets than to agree on their quality. Save perhaps twice, in the poems on the Piedmont massacre and on his deceased wife, they do not reach those heights that Shakespeare attained again and again. Milton's great achievement was to free the sonnet from the traditional characteristics of the Elizabethan sonnet both in form and content. Learned as few as his predecessors had been, he made a new beginning by turning back, direct to the fountainhead, and especially to those Italian poets of the early sixteenth century who had practiced the Italian sonnet form with subtlety and metrical variety. Thus abandoning the formal structure of the Elizabethan sonnet, which had for the most part followed Surrey and Shakespeare, Milton returned to the Italian scheme of two quatrains and two tercets. Out of this traditional form he made an English sonnet of his own. Probably because of his preference for a complex syntax rather than the simple grammatical structure of the typical Elizabethan sonnet, he more frequently than not ignored the rule for the division between octave and sestet, dissociating syntax from metrics by means of enjambement—the running over of the sense from one line to another—and once or twice not completing the thought of the octave until the twelfth line, as in "On His Deceased Wife." Milton's practice in this respect has occasioned much discussion and argument, one of his most distinguished editors lamenting that he had mistaken the nature of the Petrarchan scheme.[5] Modern views, however, doubtless influenced by the experiments in sonnet form, as in other poetic forms, which are so much a feature of twentieth-century poetry, tend to feel that such excessive demands for purity and precision are an error. Certainly the early Italians themselves did not dream of imposing such restrictions. In this matter, as in other artistic controversies, it seems wisest to cultivate a pragmatic approach, unhampered by an excess of theory. Whatever succeeds is its own justification, and Milton's sonnets are the best arguments for his practice.

His enlargement of the sonnet's traditional themes, manner, and content, however, admit of no argument. He entirely abandoned the previous fashion of the sequence. Each sonnet is separate, and only one, his earliest, is on the subject of romantic love. These are "occasional" poems in which he expresses his thoughts about people and events, the circumstances of his own life, and nature of his times, and are less purely reflective than calls to himself and others to deeds and action. Although in his conceits he often follows established conventions, Milton is free from the two marked failings of earlier sonneteers: indiscriminate borrowing and self-repetition. Tone and matter alike guard his sonnets from any tinge of the overly facile or artificial. His tone is varied, sometimes lofty, sometimes more familiar and colloquial, occasionally almost savage, but always direct, simple, and sincere. He replaces the vagueness of thought and the verbal luxuriance of the Elizabethans with classical restraint and precision of image and diction. His care and skill for the music of word and phrase lend his sonnets a sonority of orchestration unknown to any but the greatest of his predecessors. And, like his longer poems, his sonnets exhibit his characteristic mixture and interpenetration of classical, biblical, medieval, Renaissance, and Puritan traditions. "Milton's position among the writers of the sonnet . . . is due to his greatness as a poet, the wide compass of his powers, the extent of his reading, his many-sided character, and his interest in life, literature, society, politics, and religion."[6] With him, the sonnet virtually disappeared from English poetry for nearly a hundred years, to rise again after an age of satire and of prose with the pre-Romantic poets of the late eighteenth century.

[5] Mark Pattison, *The Sonnets of John Milton* (London, 1883).

[6] John S. Smart, *The Sonnets of Milton* (Glasgow, 1921), p. 42.

Sir Thomas Wyatt (1503?–1542)

"The long love that in my thought I harbor"

A remarkably close translation of Petrarch's "Amor, che nel penser mio vive e regna," which should be compared with Surrey's somewhat later version of the same sonnet (p. 18). Wyatt's poem reveals his preference for the careful, logical working out of a conceit rather than a more imaginative, emotional approach. On first reading, in fact, the thought is difficult to follow, depending as it does on feudal relationships and concepts as well as on the conventions of courtly love. Love has taken the lover captive and resides in his heart. He now causes the lady's displeasure by displaying himself openly in the lover's face, whereas courtly love enjoined concealment. Fearing her resentment, love then flees "to the heart's forest" to hide himself again. The lover, invoking the feudal principle of life and death loyalty to the liege lord, resolves to remain faithful to love, his master. The relationship depicted is a kind of triangle: the lover's devotion to his mistress is the service of love himself, imagined as a feudal lord.

Technically, the poem shows Wyatt's change to a couplet ending from the more usual form of the Italian sestet, and his difficulty in suiting meter to accent, hampered as he was early in the century by an unsettled technique and an unsettled language. Surrey's sonnet shows his advance in mastery of versification and his abandonment of the rhyme scheme of the Italian sonnet for the form that Shakespeare was to make famous.

> The long love that in my thought I harbor,
> And in my heart doth keep his residence,
> Into my face presseth with bold pretense
> And there campeth, displaying his banner.
> She that me learns to love and to suffer
> And wills that my trust and lust's negligence
> Be reigned by reason, shame, and reverence,

With his hardiness takes displeäsure.
Wherewith love to the heart's forest he fleeth,
Leaving his enterprise with pain and cry,
And there him hideth, and not appeareth:
What may I do when my master feareth
But in the field with him to live and die?
For good is the life ending faithfully.

"I find no peace, and all my war is done"

Compare with Surrey's "Vow to Love Faithfully, Howsoever He Be Rewarded" (p. 18). Both illustrate the delight that imitators of Petrarch took in exaggeration, in contradiction, and in paradox. The "contrarious passions" of the lover are in the best traditions of courtly love.

I find no peace, and all my war is done;
I fear and hope; I burn, and freeze like ice;
I fly aloft, yet can I not arise;
And nought I have, and all the world I season.
That locks nor looseth holdeth me in prison,
And holds me not, yet can I 'scape no wise;
Nor lets me live, nor die, at my devise,
And yet of death it giveth me occasion.
Without eye, I see; without tongue, I plain;
I wish to perish, yet I ask for health;
I love another, and thus I hate myself;
I feed me in sorrow, and laugh in all my pain.
Lo, thus displeaseth me both death and life,
And my delight is causer of this strife.

A Renouncing of Love

This sonnet proclaims manly independence and freedom from the power of love, which in a succession of shifting images is at one and the same time a grave judge binding by edict, a crafty fisherman

hoping to entangle the soul with "baited hooks," and finally a
delusive tree with "rotten boughs."

> Farewell, love, and all thy laws for ever,
> Thy baited hooks shall tangle me no more;
> Senec and Plato call me from thy lore
> To perfect wealth, my wit for to endeavor;
> In blindë error when I did persëver,
> Thy sharp repulse that pricketh aye so sore
> Taught me in trifles that I set no store,
> But scape forth thence, since liberty is lever.
> Therefore, farewell! Go trouble younger hearts,
> And in me claim no more authority;
> With idle youth go use thy property,
> And thereon spend thy many brittle darts.
> For hitherto though I have lost my time,
> Me list no longer rotten boughs to climb.

Henry Howard, Earl of Surrey (1517?–1547)

Description of Spring

Surrey's most charming and individual treatment of the
Petrarchan tradition is less abstract and intellectual than Wyatt's.
It is full of real, observed detail and the signs and portents of an
English spring. It is also more attentive to craftsmanship: the
regularity of meter and cadence is reinforced by sound effects, by
alliteration and the music of liquid consonants—l's, s's, and w's—
and by the repetitious rhyme scheme.

> The soote season that bud and bloom forth brings
> With green hath clad the hill and eke the vale,
> The nightingale with feathers new she sings,
> The turtle to her make hath told her tale.
> Summer is come, for every spray now springs,

The hart hath hung his old head on the pale,
The buck in brake his winter coat he flings,
The fishes float with new repairëd scale,
The adder all her slough away she slings,
The swift swallow pursueth the flyës smale,
The busy bee her honey now she mings,—
Winter is worn, that was the flowers' bale:
And thus I see, among these pleasant things
Each care decays—and yet my sorrow springs.

Complaint of a Lover Rebuked

Love that liveth and reigneth in my thought,
That built his seat within my captive breast,
Clad in the arms wherein with me he fought,
Oft in my face he doth his banner rest.
She that me taught to love and suffer pain,
My doubtful hope and eke my hot desire
With shamefast cloak to shadow and refrain,
Her smiling grace converteth straight to ire;
And coward love then to the heart apace
Taketh his flight, whereas he lurks and plains
His purpose lost, and dare not show his face.
For my lord's guilt thus faultless bide I pains;
Yet from my lord shall not my foot remove,—
Sweet is his death that takes his end by love.

Vow to Love Faithfully, Howsoever He Be Rewarded

Set me whereas the sun doth parch the green,
Or where his beams do not dissolve the ice,
In temperate heat where he is felt and seen;
In presence prest of people, mad or wise;
Set me in high or yet in low degree,
In longest night or in the shortest day,
In clearest sky or where clouds thickest be,

In lusty youth or when my hairs are gray.
Set me in heaven, in earth, or else in hell;
In hill, or dale, or in the foaming flood;
Thrall or at large, alive whereso I dwell,
Sick or in health, in evil fame or good:
Hers will I be, and only with this thought
Content myself although my chance be nought.

Edmund Spenser (1552?–1599)

FROM *Amoretti*

9–"Long-while I sought to what I might compare"

*An example of Spenser's elevation of thought and feeling and his
use, at once traditional and individual, of the Petrarchan conceits.
Here the conventional comparisons are invoked only to be rejected
and the lady's beauty is celebrated not for its own sake but for
the divine light and loveliness it reflects.*

Long-while I sought to what I might compare
Those powerful eyes, which lighten my dark spright;
Yet find I naught on earth, to which I dare
Resemble th' image of their goodly light.
Not to the Sun; for they do shine by night;
Nor to the Moon; for they are changed never;
Nor to the Stars; for they have purer sight;
Nor to the Fire; for they consume not ever;
Nor to the Lightning; for they still perséver;
Nor to the Diamond; for they are more tender;
Nor unto Crystal; for nought may them sever;
Nor unto Glass; such, baseness mought offend her.
   Then to the Maker self they likest be,
    Whose light doth lighten all that here we see.

15–"Ye tradeful Merchants, that, with weary toil"

A conventional Petrarchan sonnet, praising the lady's physical charms but implying that through worship of the body the lover is led to knowledge and worship on a higher, more spiritual plane. In the traditional Platonic manner, he ascends from flesh to soul.

Ye tradeful Merchants, that, with weary toil,
Do seek most precious things to make your gain;
And both the Indias of their treasure spoil;
What needeth you to seek so far in vain?
For lo, my love doth in her self contain
All this world's riches that may far be found:
If sapphires, lo, her eyes be sapphires plain;
If rubies, lo, her lips be rubies sound;
If pearls, her teeth be pearls, both pure and round;
If ivory, her forehead ivory ween;
If gold, her locks are finest gold on ground;
If silver, her fair hands are silver sheen:
    But that which fairest is, but few behold,
    Her mind adorned with virtues manifold.

65–"One day I wrote her name upon the strand"

The "eternizing" theme, given individual expression by the use of dialogue between lady and lover. Spenser thus converts the more usual boast of the poet into a graceful compliment to his love.

One day I wrote her name upon the strand,
    But came the waves and washèd it away:
Again I wrote it with a second hand,
    But came the tide and made my pains his prey.
    Vain man (said she), that dost in vain assay
A mortal thing so to immortalise;
    For I myself shall like to this decay,
And eke my name be wipèd out likewise.

Not so (quod I); let baser things devise
　To die in dust, but you shall live by fame;
My verse your virtues rare shall eternise,
　And in the heavens write your glorious name:
　　Where, whenas Death shall all the world subdue,
　　Our love shall live, and later life renew.

68–Easter

*Spenser's noblest statement of the correspondence of human to
divine love. Astrophel struggles with his passion for Stella and
finally turns to "higher things"; Shakespeare's passion seems to
him "the expense of spirit in a waste of shame," a hell he cannot
shun; Spenser, celebrating virtuous courtship, sees his love for a
woman linked with, and leading to, love of God.*

Most glorious Lord of life! that on this day
　Didst make thy triumph over death and sin,
And having harrowed hell didst bring away
　Captivity thence captive, us to win:
　This joyous day, dear Lord, with joy begin;
And grant that we, for whom Thou diddest die,
　Being with thy dear blood clean washed from sin,
May live for ever in felicity,
And that thy love we weighing worthily,
　May likewise love Thee for the same again;
And for thy sake, that all like dear didst buy,
　With love may one another entertain.
　　So let us love, dear Love, like as we ought:
　　Love is the lesson which the Lord us taught.

70–"Fresh Spring, the herald of Love's mighty King"

*The "gather ye rosebuds" theme so common in Renaissance poetry.
Spenser employs the conventional imagery of spring to suggest
both the beauty and brevity of love.*

Fresh Spring, the herald of Love's mighty King,
  In whose cote-armour richly are display'd
All sorts of flowers the which on earth do spring
  In goodly colours gloriously array'd,—
  Go to my Love, where she is careless laid
Yet in her Winter's bower not well awake:
  Tell her the joyous time will not be stay'd
Unless she do him by the fore-lock take:
Bid her therefore herself soon ready make:
  To wait on Love amongst his lovely crew:
Where every one that misseth then her make,
  Shall be by him amerced with penance due.
    Make haste therefore, sweet Love, whilst it is prime,
    For none can call again the passèd time.

83–"Let not one spark of filthy lustful fire"

*Oddly enough, this sonnet seems more suggestive in its rejection
of "filthy lustful fire" than a forthright declaration of passion. The
lover, himself denied the sight of the lady's charms, sends in his
place "pure affections" and "modest thoughts" to visit her in
"her chaste bower of rest," bidding them to "behold her rare
perfection." Clearly it is only his sight, not his imagination,
that is deprived of sensual pleasure.*

Let not one spark of filthy lustful fire
Break out, that may her sacred peace molest;
Ne one light glance of sensual desire
Attempt to work her gentle mind's unrest:
But pure affections bred in spotless breast,
And modest thoughts breath'd from well-tempered sprites,
Go visit her in her chaste bower of rest
Accompanied with angel-like delights.
There fill yourself with those most joyous sights,
The which myself could never yet attain:
But speak no word to her of these sad plights,
Which her too constant stiffness doth constrain.

Only behold her rare perfection,
And bless your fortune's fair election.

Sir Walter Raleigh (1552–1618)

A Vision Upon This Conceit of the Fairy Queen

*A tribute to the Petrarchan tradition and to Queen Elizabeth, the
"Faery Queen." Her fame, celebrated like that of Laura by a great
poet, has deprived Laura's tomb of its attendants, Love and Virtue,
who desert it to attend the living Queen. Since its beginning the
sonnet has frequently been used, as this one is, for purposes of
compliment. In its opening phrase we hear the later and better
known lines of "On His Deceased Wife" of Milton (p. 61). The
poem is, however, English or Shakespearean in form, like
the majority of Elizabethan sonnets.*

Methought I saw the grave where Laura lay,
Within that temple where the vestal flame
Was wont to burn; and passing by that way
To see that buried dust of living fame,
Whose tomb fair Love and fairer Virtue kept,
All suddenly I saw the Fairy Queen;
At whose approach the soul of Petrarch wept,
And from thenceforth those graces were not seen,
For they this Queen attended; in whose stead
Oblivion laid him down on Laura's hearse.
Hereat the hardest stones were seen to bleed,
And groans of buried ghosts the heavens did pierce;
   Where Homer's sprite did tremble all for grief,
   And cursed th' access of that celestial thief.

Sir Philip Sidney (1554–1586)

*Sidney's sonnets are a curious mixture of the conventional and the
highly individual. Their themes and images were already
traditional: they declare the lover's devotion and constancy; lament
his mistress's cruelty; compliment her beauty; chronicle the conflict
of sensual love with virtue; and eventually record the triumph of
the latter. They invoke the moon, herself a victim of Cupid's
arrows, who, since she loved the mortal Endymion, must feel "a
lover's case"; they summon sleep to end the lover's woe; they
employ all the usual hyperbolic comparisons and conceits. But
their diction is plain, vigorous, and often colloquial; and the voice
that speaks in them is a man's living voice.*

FROM *Astrophel and Stella*

31–"With how sad steps, O moon, . . ."

With how sad steps, O moon, thou climb'st the skies!
How silently, and with how wan a face!
What! may it be that even in heav'nly place
That busy archer his sharp arrows tries?
Sure, if that long-with-love-acquainted eyes
Can judge of love, thou feel'st a lover's case;
I read it in thy looks,—thy languished grace
To me, that feel the like, thy state descries.
Then, ev'n of fellowship, O moon, tell me,
Is constant love deemed there but want of wit?
Are beauties there as proud as here they be?
Do they above love to be loved, and yet
Those lovers scorn whom that love doth possess?
Do they call virtue there ungratefulness?

39–"Come sleep! O sleep . . ."

Come sleep! O sleep, the certain knot of peace,
  The baiting place of wit, the balm of woe,
  The poor man's wealth, the prisoner's release,
  Th' indifferent judge between the high and low;
With shield of proof shield me from out the prease
  Of those fierce darts despair at me doth throw;
  O make in me those civil wars to cease;
  I will good tribute pay, if thou do so.
Take thou of me smooth pillows, sweetest bed,
  A chamber deaf to noise and blind to light,
  A rosy garland and a weary head;
And if these things, as being thine by right,
  Move not thy heavy grace, thou shalt in me,
  Livelier than elsewhere, Stella's image see.

54–"Because I breathe not love to every one"

*A demonstration of Sidney's skill in managing dialogue in a
manner both natural and dramatic and the high spirits of a man
who can reject the conventional behavior of a lover even while he
affirms the sincerity of his devotion.*

Because I breathe not love to every one,
  Nor do not use set colors for to wear,
  Nor nourish special locks of vowèd hair,
  Nor give each speech a full point of a groan,
The courtly nymphs, acquainted with the moan
  Of them who in their lips Love's standard bear,
  What, he! say they of me, Now I dare swear
  He cannot love; no, no, let him alone.
And think so still, so Stella know my mind;
  Profess indeed I do not Cupid's art;
  But you, fair maids, at length this true shall find,

That his right badge is but worn in the heart;
  Dumb swans, not chatt'ring pies, do lovers prove;
  They love indeed who quake to say they love.

64–"No more, my dear . . ."

No more, my dear, no more these counsels try;
  Oh, give my passions leave to run their race;
  Let fortune lay on me her worst disgrace;
  Let folk o'ercharged with brain against me cry;
Let clouds bedim my face, break in mine eye;
  Let me no steps but of lost labor trace;
  Let all the earth with scorn recount my case,
  But do not will me from my love to fly.
I do not envy Aristotle's wit,
  Nor do aspire to Cæsar's bleeding fame;
  Nor aught do care though some above me sit;
Nor hope nor wish another course to frame,
  But that which once may win thy cruel heart;
  Thou art my wit, and thou my virtue art.

*Sidney's two finest sonnets, "Thou blind man's mark . . ." and
"Leave me, O love . . . ," show different aspects of his many-sided
personality and his technical skill. The former is characterized by a
vigor, almost a violence, of diction and image, reinforced by its
abrupt, muscular rhythms and effective use of repetition. The latter
combines phrases reminiscent of Scripture and particularly of the
Book of Common Prayer—"that which never taketh rust," "that
sweet yoke where lasting freedoms be," "the light,/That doth both
shine and give us sight to see"—with Christian feeling and an
elevation of mood and tone that make it one of the noblest sonnets
ever written. Sidney's most characteristic rhyme scheme, like
that of Wyatt, is hybrid in form, combining the Italian octave
a b b a a b b a, with a sestet ending with a rhyming couplet
c d c d e e. He employs numerous variations, though only once,
in "Leave me, O love . . . ," did he use the English form.*

"Thou blind man's mark . . ."

Thou blind man's mark, thou fool's self-chosen snare,
Fond fancy's scum, and dregs of scattered thought;
Band of all evils, cradle of causeless care;
Thou web of will, whose end is never wrought;
Desire, desire! I have too dearly bought,
With price of mangled mind, thy worthless ware;
Too long, too long, asleep thou hast me brought,
Who should my mind to higher things prepare.
But yet in vain thou hast my ruin sought;
In vain thou madest me to vain things aspire;
In vain thou kindlest all thy smoky fire;
For virtue hath this better lesson taught,—
Within myself to seek my only hire,
Desiring nought but how to kill desire.

"Leave me, O love . . ."

Leave me, O love which reachest but to dust;
And thou, my mind, aspire to higher things;
Grow rich in that which never taketh rust,
Whatever fades but fading pleasure brings.
Draw in thy beams, and humble all thy might
To that sweet yoke where lasting freedoms be;
Which breaks the clouds and opens forth the light,
That doth both shine and give us sight to see.
O take fast hold; let that light be thy guide
In this small course which birth draws out to death,
And think how evil becometh him to slide,
Who seeketh heav'n, and comes of heav'nly breath.
   Then farewell, world; thy uttermost I see;
   Eternal Love, maintain thy life in me.

Splendidis longum valedico nugis.

Henry Constable (1562–1613)

"My lady's presence makes the roses red"

This sonnet shows Constable using imagery exploited in literally hundreds of sonnets of this period—but with a difference. Here, the lady's beauty and the passion and pain of her lover not only communicate their virtue to the beauties of nature, but become the very principle of life and growth. What is usually only a pretty, ingenious conceit is raised almost to the stature of myth.

My lady's presence makes the roses red,
  Because to see her lips they blush with shame.
  The lily's leaves for envy pale became,
And her white hands in them this envy bred.
The marigold the leaves abroad doth spread,
  Because the sun's and her power is the same.
  The violet of purple colour came,
Dyed in the blood she made my heart to shed.
  In brief, all flowers from her their virtue take;
From her sweet breath their sweet smells do proceed;
  The living heat which her eyebeams doth make
Warmeth the ground and quickeneth the seed.
  The rain wherewith she watereth the flowers,
  Falls from mine eyes which she dissolves in showers.

Samuel Daniel (1562?–1619)

"Beauty, sweet love, is like the morning dew"

Beginning placidly with a conventional comparison of the lady's beauty to that of nature, this sonnet deepens in tone to a sobering reminder of death, and then closes with a sudden and surprising turn of mood. The combinations of passion and praise and of playful mockery and grim warning anticipate in mood, if not in structure, Marvell's later and more famous "To His Coy Mistress." Note in all three sonnets the devices Daniel used to lighten and vary his meter and make it fluid in movement: the mixture of feminine rhymes with the more usual masculine ones as well as the half or consonant rhymes—dew/show, alone/gone—*along with true rhymes.*

> Beauty, sweet love, is like the morning dew,
>   Whose short refresh upon the tender green
>   Cheers for a time but till the sun doth show,
>   And straight 'tis gone as it had never been.
> Soon doth it fade that makes the fairest flourish,
>   Short is the glory of the blushing rose,
>   The hue which thou so carefully dost nourish,
>   Yet which at length thou must be forced to lose.
> When thou, surcharged with burden of thy years,
>   Shalt bend thy wrinkles homeward to the earth,
>   And that in beauty's lease expired appears
>   The date of age, the kalends of our death,—
> But ah! no more, this must not be foretold,
> For women grieve to think they must be old.

"When men shall find thy flower . . ."

The following sonnet is Shakespearean in the intensity and pride with which it proclaims the transitoriness of beauty, and the constancy of love.

> When men shall find thy flower, thy glory, pass,
>   And thou with careful brow sitting alone,
>   Receivëd hast this message from thy glass,
>   That tells the truth and says that all is gone;
> Fresh shalt thou see in me the wounds thou mad'st,
>   Though spent thy flame, in me the heat remaining;
>   I that have loved thee thus before thou fad'st,

My faith shall wax when thou art in thy waning.
The world shall find this miracle in me,
   That fire can burn when all the matter's spent;
   Then what my faith hath been, thyself shall see,
   And that thou wast unkind, thou mayst repent.
Thou mayst repent that thou hast scorned my tears,
When winter snows upon thy sable hairs.

"Care-charmer sleep . . ."

A depth of feeling, conveyed both in image and diction,
distinguish this poem from Sidney's more graceful, less poignant
statement of the same theme (p. 25).

Care-charmer sleep, son of the sable night,
   Brother to death, in silent darkness born,
   Relieve my languish and restore the light;
   With dark forgetting of my care, return.
And let the day be time enough to mourn
   The shipwreck of my ill-adventured youth;
   Let waking eyes suffice to wail their scorn
   Without the torment of the night's untruth.
Cease, dreams, th' images of day-desires,
   To model forth the passions of the morrow;
   Never let rising sun approve you liars,
   To add more grief to aggravate my sorrow.
Still let me sleep, embracing clouds in vain,
And never wake to feel the day's disdain.

Michael Drayton (1563–1631)

"Dear, why should you command me to my rest"

A variation on the more usual summons of sleep to end the lover's

*pain. Its gentle diction and graceful, unimpassioned declaration of
love stand in sharp contrast with two of Drayton's other sonnets.*

Dear, why should you command me to my rest,
When now the night doth summon all to sleep?
Methinks this time becometh lovers best;
Night was ordained together friends to keep.
How happy are all other living things,
Which though the day disjoin by sev'ral flight,
The quiet evening yet together brings,
And each returns unto his love at night!
O thou that art so courteous else to all,
Why shouldst thou, Night, abuse me only thus,
That ev'ry creature to his kind dost call,
And yet 'tis thou dost only sever us?
    Well could I wish it would be ever day,
    If when night comes you bid me go away.

"How many paltry, foolish, painted things"

*The following sonnet takes its energy and conviction from the pride
and scorn of a poet rather than from the passion of a lover.*

How many paltry, foolish, painted things,
That now in coaches trouble ev'ry street,
Shall be forgotten, whom no poet sings,
Ere they be well wrapped in their winding sheet!
Where I to thee eternity shall give,
When nothing else remaineth of these days,
And queens hereafter shall be glad to live
Upon the alms of thy superfluous praise;
Virgins and matrons reading these my rhymes
Shall be so much delighted with thy story
That they shall grieve they lived not in these times,
To have seen thee, their sex's only glory.
    So shalt thou fly above the vulgar throng,
    Still to survive in my immortal song.

"Since there's no help, come let us kiss and part"

*Immortality conferred not upon a mistress but upon the poet.
Here the conflict between the slavery of love and the desire for
independence, between passion and pride, achieves its most
memorable utterance. Aside from Shakespeare's poems, only one
other sonnet on the power and constancy of love, Joshua Sylvester's
"Were I as base as is the lowly plain" (p. 33) is worthy to
stand beside it.*

Since there's no help, come let us kiss and part;
Nay, I have done, you get no more of me,
And I am glad, yea glad with all my heart
That thus so cleanly I myself can free;
Shake hands forever, cancel all our vows,
And when we meet at any time again,
Be it not seen in either of our brows
That we one jot of former love retain.
Now at the last gasp of love's latest breath,
When, his pulse failing, passion speechless lies,
When faith is kneeling by his bed of death,
And innocence is closing up his eyes,
    Now if thou wouldst, when all have given him over,
    From death to life thou mightst him yet recover.

Giles Fletcher (1549?–1611)

"In time the strong and stately turrets fall"

*Of the sonnets here, Giles Fletcher's is perhaps most typical of
the period. However, it surpasses the majority of them in
the grace and skill with which it uses conventional comparisons
drawn from nature for purposes of compliment. The repeated*

tolling of the phrase in time *throughout the poem points up with particular effectiveness the final declaration of the durability of beauty, virtue, and love.*

> In time the strong and stately turrets fall,
> In time the rose and silver lilies die,
> In time the monarchs captive are, and thrall,
> In time the sea and rivers are made dry;
> The hardest flint in time doth melt asunder;
> Still-living fame in time doth fade away;
> The mountains proud we see in time come under;
> And earth, for age, we see in time decay.
> The sun in time forgets for to retire
> From out the east where he was wont to rise;
> The basest thoughts we see in time aspire,
> And greedy minds in time do wealth despise.
>   Thus all, sweet fair, in time must have an end,
>   Except thy beauty, virtues, and thy friend.

Joshua Sylvester (1563–1618)

"Were I as base as is the lowly plain"

Known today to most readers only by this one poem, Sylvester takes his place as a sonneteer with the greatest. The conventional hyperboles and conceits in this sonnet for once shame convention into sincerity, and the utter simplicity of its ending is as much beyond comment as it is beyond praise.

> Were I as base as is the lowly plain,
> And you, my love, as high as heav'n above,
> Yet should the thoughts of me, your humble swain,
> Ascend to heaven in honor of my love.
> Were I as high as heav'n above the plain,
> And you, my love, as humble and as low

As are the deepest bottoms of the main,
Wheresoe'er you were, with you my love should go.
Were you the earth, dear love, and I the skies,
My love should shine on you like to the sun,
And look upon you with ten thousand eyes,
Till heaven waxed blind and till the world were dun.
   Wheresoe'er I am, below, or else above you,
   Wheresoe'er you are, my heart shall truly love you.

Fulke Greville, Baron Brooke (1554–1628)

"The earth with thunder torn . . ."

*Occasionally—very occasionally—the sonnets of this period cast off
the livery of Venus and donned that of Minerva. Fulke Greville
was Sidney's close friend, born in the same year though outliving
Sidney by more than forty years. "The earth with thunder torn . . ."
shows a strain recurrent in the sonnet at all periods: philosophical
rather than Petrarchan, intellectual in design rather than imaginative
or emotional, employing an argument by analogy to present a
Stoic view of the human condition whose constant struggle and
sorrow can only be endured.*

The earth with thunder torn, with fire blasted,
With waters drowned, with windy palsy shaken,
Cannot for this with heaven be distasted,
Since thunder, rain, and winds from earth are taken;
Man torn with love, with inward furies blasted,
Drowned with despair, with fleshly lustings shaken,
Cannot for this with heaven be distasted;
Love, fury, lustings out of man are taken.
Then, man, endure thyself, those clouds will vanish;
Life is a top which whipping sorrow driveth;
Wisdom must bear what our flesh cannot banish.
The humble lead, the stubborn bootless striveth.

Or, man, forsake thyself, to heaven turn thee,
Her flames enlighten nature, never burn thee.

Barnabe Barnes (1569?–1609)

Content

Greville's energy of diction and of thought contrasts strikingly with the tranquil simplicity of Barnes' sonnet "Content." Here, the three quatrains are linked rhetorically by skillful repetition of key phrases rather than by logic, and the simple diction and syntax and smooth, fluid movement and sound patterns are almost hypnotically soothing, in paradoxical opposition to the stated thought.

Ah, sweet Content! where is thy mild abode?
  Is it with shepherds and light-hearted swains
Which sing upon the downs and pipe abroad,
  Tending their flocks and cattle on the plains?
Ah, sweet Content! where dost thou safely rest?
  In heaven, with angels which the praises sing
Of Him that made, and rules at his behest,
  The minds and hearts of every living thing?
Ah, sweet Content! where doth thine harbour hold?
  Is it in churches with religious men
Which please the gods with prayers manifold,
  And in their studies meditate it then?—
    Whether thou dost in heaven or earth appear,
    Be where thou wilt, thou will not harbour here.

William Drummond of Hawthornden (1585–1649)

"A good that never satisfies the mind"

Drummond's "A good that never satisfies the mind" shows the poet piling up comparisons and paradoxes in the conventional manner, but here these conceits are used not to praise beauty, command love, or celebrate the power of verse, but to persuade the rational mind to despise life and prepare for death. The argument is reinforced by repetition in phrase and in rhyme scheme; with theme, structure, and sound chiming together like a passing bell, the mood is melancholy rather than resigned.

> A good that never satisfies the mind,
> A beauty fading like the April flowers,
> A sweet with floods of gall that runs combined,
> A pleasure passing ere in thought made ours,
> A honor that more fickle is than wind,
> A glory at opinion's frown that lours,
> A treasury which bankrupt time devours,
> A knowledge than grave ignorance more blind,
> A vain delight our equals to command,
> A style of greatness, in effect a dream,
> A fabulous thought of holding sea and land,
> A servile lot, decked with a pompous name,
>   Are the strange ends we toil for here below,
>   Till wisest death make us our errors know.

"I know that all beneath the moon decays"

"I know that all beneath the moon decays" is remarkable for the power and grandeur of its survey of a transitory world and the

abrupt, unexpected turn with which it comes to a rueful, almost
humorous, conclusion.

> I know that all beneath the moon decays,
> And what by mortals in this world is brought
> In time's great periods shall return to nought;
> That fairest states have fatal nights and days.
> I know how all the muses' heavenly lays,
> With toil of sprite which are so dearly bought,
> As idle sounds of few or none are sought,
> And that nought lighter is than airy praise.
> I know frail beauty, like the purple flower
> To which one morn oft birth and death affords;
> That love a jarring is of minds' accords,
> Where sense and will invassal reason's power;
> > Know what I list, this all can not me move,
> > But that, oh me, I both must write and love!

William Shakespeare (1564–1616)

A careful reading of Shakespeare's sonnets will reveal at once his
likeness and his superiority to his contemporaries. The familiar
themes—beauty, love, mutability, the power of verse—are presented
in metaphors that are logical, precise, and rich in imaginative,
suggestive power; in diction both simple and stately; and
thought, mood, and metaphor are bound together and reinforced
by patterns of sound, rhythm, and cadence. Powerful oppositions
are made vivid through sharp contrasts: youth and age, spring and
fall, day and night, past and present, present and future, beauty and
decay, art and nature, love and time, body and soul; and the
contrasts are dramatized in concrete images. The mood, too, is
complex and ambivalent, pride and passion coexisting with self-
effacement and humility, joy with pain, celebration with re-
nunciation.

12–"When I do count the clock that tells the time"

*Words and images weave back and forth, echoing against one
another to paint the picture, in sensuous and poignant terms,
of a world of process. The violet past its prime, an image of beauty's
decay, is both compared and contrasted with "summer's green
all girded up in sheaves/Borne on the bier with white and bristly
beard:"—a more concrete and human image of old age and death,
with the additional suggestion that summer's green has served its
natural function, has produced "breed" in its sheaves. Sable curls
are black as "hideous night"; but the black curls, paradoxically, are
the emblems of the "brave day" of youth and beauty, and their
silvering o'er, lovely and bright in itself, signals death as clearly as
the white beard of the gathered grain. Strength and function,
like youth and beauty, pass: "lofty trees I see barren of leaves,/
Which erst from heat did canopy the herd"; but exercised in their
prime they enable beauty to replenish itself, and cheat Time, the
condition of nature. Sound patterns too—simple but not obtrusive
alliteration, assonance, consonance—echo from line to line; the soft
melody of the s's, l's, w's, and th's is counterpointed by the hard,
sharp b's, d's, g's, t's. Sonnets 15, 18, and 60 present the same picture
of a world of process in which youth and beauty are caught up
like all natural things, where time, which only love and art can
combat, will bring both fruition and decay.*

When I do count the clock that tells the time,
And see the brave day sunk in hideous night;
When I behold the violet past prime,
And sable curls all silver'd o'er with white;
When lofty trees I see barren of leaves,
Which erst from heat did canopy the herd,
And summer's green all girded up in sheaves
Borne on the bier with white and bristly beard,
Then of thy beauty do I question make,
That thou among the wastes of time must go,
Since sweets and beauties do themselves forsake
And die as fast they see others grow;

And nothing 'gainst Time's scythe can make defence
Save breed, to brave him when he takes thee hence.

15–"When I consider everything that grows"

Unlike the previous one, this sonnet builds by a series of abstract
statements instead of concrete images until the final line, when
"ingraft" suddenly condenses the total sonnet into one word:
the poet in his verse, like a skillful and devoted gardener in the
world of nature, will by his art preserve the youthful beauty of his
friend far past its early day.

When I consider every thing that grows
Holds in perfection but a little moment,
That this huge stage presenteth naught but shows
Whereon the stars in secret influence comment;
When I perceive that men as plants increase,
Cheer'd and check'd even by the selfsame sky,
Vaunt in their youthful sap, at height decrease,
And wear their brave state out of memory:
Then the conceit of this inconstant stay
Sets you most rich in youth before my sight,
Where wasteful Time debateth with Decay
To change your day of youth to sullied night;
    And all in war with Time for love of you,
    As he takes from you, I ingraft you new.

18–"Shall I compare thee to a summer's day?"

Shall I compare thee to a summer's day?
Thou art more lovely and more temperate:
Rough winds do shake the darling buds of May,
And summer's lease hath all too short a date:
Sometime too hot the eye of heaven shines,
And often is his gold complexion dimm'd;
And every fair from fair sometimes declines,
By chance, or nature's changing course, untrimm'd;

But thy eternal summer shall not fade
Nor lose possession of that fair thou ow'st,
Nor shall Death brag thou wand'rest in his shade
When in eternal lines to time thou grow'st:
  So long as men can breathe or eyes can see,
  So long lives this, and this gives life to thee.

29–"When in disgrace with fortune and men's eyes"

When in disgrace with fortune and men's eyes,
I all alone beweep my outcast state,
And trouble deaf heaven with my bootless cries,
And look upon myself and curse my fate,
Wishing me like to one more rich in hope,
Featur'd like him, like him with friends possess'd,
Desiring this man's art, and that man's scope,
With what I most enjoy contented least;
Yet in these thoughts myself almost despising,
Haply I think on thee, and then my state,
Like to the lark at break of day arising
From sullen earth, sings hymns at heaven's gate;
  For thy sweet love rememb'red such wealth brings
  That then I scorn to change my state with kings.

30–"When to the sessions of sweet silent thought"

At times, anguish, pride, and passion yield to softer moods. The humility of a lover replaces the arrogance of the artist, and the poet puts himself at love's service and declares it a compensation for all grief and all failure. In sonnet 30 humility, grief, and tenderness are expressed with a seductive sweetness of sound and cadence. Paradoxically, this most exquisitely personal and moving of love poems employs the central figure of a legal hearing, and balances love and loss against each other in a kind of debits and credits statement. The aging poet, like a court bailiff, "summons" his memories to the "sessions" of thought, mourning afresh the "long since cancelled" woes in his personal ledgers and paying afresh

long since paid accounts. But his conclusion is that love is the
decisive entry and compensates for all losses.

When to the sessions of sweet silent thought
I summon up remembrance of things past,
I sigh the lack of many a thing I sought
And with old woes new wail my dear time's waste;
Then can I drown an eye unus'd to flow,
For precious friends hid in death's dateless night,
And weep afresh love's long since cancell'd woe,
And moan th' expense of many a vanish'd sight;
Then can I grieve at grievances foregone,
And heavily from woe to woe tell o'er
The sad account of fore-bemoaned moan,
Which I new pay as if not paid before:
    But if the while I think on thee, dear friend,
    All losses are restor'd and sorrows end.

33–"Full many a glorious morning have I seen"

The beloved is the sun of the lover's world, illuminating him as
the sun itself does the world of nature. Just as, in the inconstancy of
nature, the sun is often hidden by clouds, so the inconstancy of
the beloved has masked him from the lover's view. Yet, even while
he declares love to be as changing as the world of nature, the poet
affirms the constancy of his own love.

Full many a glorious morning have I seen
Flatter the mountain tops with sovereign eye,
Kissing with golden face the meadows green,
Gilding pale streams with heavenly alchemy;
Anon permit the basest clouds to ride
With ugly rack on his celestial face
And from the forlorn world his visage hide,
Stealing unseen to west with this disgrace:
Even so my sun one early morn did shine
With all triumphant splendour on my brow;
But out alack! he was but one hour mine,

The region cloud hath mask'd him from me now.
> Yet him for this my love no whit disdaineth;
> Suns of the world may stain when heaven's sun staineth.

55–"Not marble nor the gilded monuments"

*In this sonnet the loving power of poetry will keep the lover's
beauty brighter than gilded monuments that Time, like a sluttish
servant, will smear with dust; brighter than the destructive fires
of men's wars. Like the princes whom the gilded monuments honor,
the lover shall pace forth forever in the presence of those envious
and malignant courtiers Death and Time, immortal in verse on earth
until judgment day shall bring immortality itself and an end to
Time and Death.*

Not marble nor the gilded monuments
Of princes shall outlive this pow'rful rhyme,
But you shall shine more bright in these contents
Than unswept stone, besmear'd with sluttish time.
When wasteful war shall statues overturn,
And broils root out the work of masonry,
Nor Mars his sword nor war's quick fire shall burn
The living record of your memory.
'Gainst death and all oblivious enmity
Shall you pace forth, your praise shall still find room
Even in the eyes of all posterity
That wear this world out to the ending doom.
> So, till the judgment that yourself arise,
> You live in this, and dwell in lovers' eyes.

57–"Being your slave, what should I do but tend"

Being your slave, what should I do but tend
Upon the hours and times of your desire?
I have no precious time at all to spend,
Nor services to do, till you require.
Nor dare I chide the world-without-end hour

Whilst I, my sovereign, watch the clock for you,
Nor think the bitterness of absence sour
When you have bid your servant once adieu.
Nor dare I question with my jealous thought
Where you may be, or your affairs suppose,
But, like a sad slave, stay and think of nought
Save where you are how happy you make those.
    So true a fool is love that in your Will,
    Though you do anything, he thinks no ill.

60–"Like as the waves make towards the pebbled shore"

Like as the waves make towards the pebbled shore,
So do our minutes hasten to their end,
Each changing place with that which goes before,
In sequent toil all forwards do contend.
Nativity, once in the main of light,
Crawls to maturity, wherewith being crown'd,
Crooked eclipses 'gainst his glory fight,
And Time that gave doth now his gift confound.
Time doth transfix the flourish set on youth
And delves the parallels in beauty's brow,
Feeds on the rarities of nature's truth,
And nothing stands but for his scythe to mow:
    And yet to times in hope my verse shall stand,
    Praising thy worth, despite his cruel hand.

65–"Since brass, nor stone, nor earth, nor boundless sea"

*Abstract statement is here wedded to concrete image in a mood
of anguished rebellion set against poignant hope. The poem is
made up of a series of overwhelming antitheses and paradoxes.
In its magnificent opening the durable powers of the world
expand in one line from brass to stone to earth to boundless sea,
only to be contracted and leveled in the next breath by "sad*

mortality." With piercing pathos, beauty, "whose action is no stronger than a flower," pleads in vain with the all-triumphant rage of Time and Death. Rocks, the fortress of Nature, and gates of steel, the fortress of man, are both as helpless as "summer's honey breath" to detain Time's "swift foot." The beauty that is the treasure of Time's process will be closed in a coffin like a jewel hidden by a miser in his chest. Only a miracle, the miracle of love and art, may in a final paradox succeed where the strength of nature is helpless, and "in black ink my love may still shine bright."

Since brass, nor stone, nor earth, nor boundless sea,
But sad mortality o'er-sways their power,
How with this rage shall beauty hold a plea,
Whose action is no stronger than a flower?
O how shall summer's honey breath hold out
Against the wrackful siege of batt'ring days,
When rocks impregnable are not so stout,
Nor gates of steel so strong, but Time decays?
O fearful meditation! where, alack,
Shall Time's best jewel from Time's chest lie hid?
Or what strong hand can hold his swift foot back,
Or who his spoil of beauty can forbid?
    O none, unless this miracle have might,
    That in black ink my love may still shine bright.

66–"Tir'd with all these, for restful death I cry"

Tir'd with all these, for restful death I cry:
As to behold desert a beggar born,
And needy nothing trimm'd in jollity,
And purest faith unhappily forsworn,
And gilded honour shamefully misplac'd,
And maiden virtue rudely strumpeted,
And right perfection wrongfully disgrac'd,
And strength by limping sway disabled,
And art made tongue-tied by authority,
And folly, doctor-like, controlling skill,
And simple truth miscall'd simplicity,

And captive good attending captain ill:
>Tir'd with all these, from these would I be gone,
>Save that to die, I leave my love alone.

71–"No longer mourn for me when I am dead"

No longer mourn for me when I am dead
Than you shall hear the surly sullen bell
Give warning to the world that I am fled
From this vile world, with vilest worms to dwell:
Nay, if you read this line, remember not
The hand that writ it; for I love you so,
That I in your sweet thoughts would be forgot,
If thinking on me then should make you woe.
O! if, I say, you look upon this verse
When I, perhaps, compounded am with clay.
Do not so much as my poor name rehearse,
But let your love even with my life decay;
>Lest the wise world should look into your moan,
>And mock you with me after I am gone.

73–"That time of year thou mayst in me behold"

*The aging poet reflects on his own mortality in a series of metaphors
drawn from the world of nature: the old age and death of the
year, the old age and death of the day, and the ashes of the
dying fire.*

That time of year thou mayst in me behold
When yellow leaves, or none, or few, do hang
Upon those boughs which shake against the cold,
Bare ruin'd choirs, where late the sweet birds sang:
In me thou see'st the twilight of such day
As after sunset fadeth in the west;
Which by and by black night doth take away,
Death's second self, that seals up all in rest:
In me thou see'st the glowing of such fire,

That on the ashes of his youth doth lie,
As the death-bed whereon it must expire,
Consum'd with that which it was nourish'd by.
This thou perceiv'st, which makes thy love more strong,
To love that well which thou must leave ere long.

87–"Farewell! thou art too dear for my possessing"

When, in sonnet 87, the poet takes a sad farewell of the lover, he does so in a thoroughly worked out series of legal terms and images. The gift of love was a patent granted by error or without due cause, and is now declared void. Diction and metaphor operate with precision to supply a legal, intellectual analogy to personal situation and emotion; such terms as estimate, charter, bonds, determinate, patent, *and* misprision *at once illustrate and form an ironic contrast with the inner world of love and of pain.*

Farewell! thou art too dear for my possessing,
And like enough thou know'st thy estimate:
The charter of thy worth gives thee releasing;
My bonds in thee are all determinate.
For how do I hold thee but by thy granting,
And for that riches where is my deserving?
The cause of this fair gift in me is wanting,
And so my patent back again is swerving.
Thyself thou gav'st, thy own worth then not knowing,
Or me, to whom thou gav'st it, else mistaking;
So thy great gift, upon misprision growing,
Comes home again, on better judgment making.
Thus have I had thee as a dream doth flatter,
In sleep a king, but waking no such matter.

98–"From you have I been absent in the spring"

Reminiscent of Constable's "My lady's presence makes the roses red" (p. 28) in its conventional nature imagery. Sonnets 33 and 73 show a more individual and powerful use of the conventions.

From you have I been absent in the spring,
When proud pied April, dress'd in all his trim,
Hath put a spirit of youth in everything,
That heavy Saturn laugh'd and leapt with him.
Yet nor the lays of birds, nor the sweet smell
Of different flowers in odour and in hue,
Could make me any summer's story tell,
Or from their proud lap pluck them where they grew;
Nor did I wonder at the lily's white,
Nor praise the deep vermilion in the rose;
They were but sweet, but figures of delight
Drawn after you, you pattern of all those.
>Yet seem'd it winter still, and you away,
>As with your shadow I with these did play.

107–"Not mine own fears, nor the prophetic soul"

Not mine own fears, nor the prophetic soul
Of the wide world dreaming on things to come,
Can yet the lease of my true love control,
Suppos'd as forfeit to a confin'd doom.
The mortal moon hath her eclipse endur'd,
And the sad augurs mock their own presage;
Incertainties now crown themselves assur'd,
And peace proclaims olives of endless age.
Now with the drops of this most balmy time
My love looks fresh, and Death to me subscribes,
Since, spite of him, I'll live in this poor rhyme,
While he insults o'er dull and speechless tribes:
>And thou in this shalt find thy monument,
>When tyrants' crests and tombs of brass are spent.

116–"Let me not to the marriage of true minds"

Shakespeare's most famous statement of the power of love in a world of change. Here, love that is of the spirit rather than the body,

a "marriage of true minds," is contrasted with the world of nature
that it dominates and transcends. Guiding men through the
wilderness of the world, such love is the pole star of the soul.

Let me not to the marriage of true minds
Admit impediments. Love is not love
Which alters when it alteration finds,
Or bends with the remover to remove:
O no! it is an ever fixed mark,
That looks on tempests and is never shaken;
It is the star to every wandering bark,
Whose worth's unknown, although his height be taken.
Love's not Time's fool, though rosy lips and cheeks
Within his bending sickle's compass come;
Love alters not with his brief hours and weeks,
But bears it out even to the edge of doom:
　　If this be error and upon me proved,
　　I never writ, nor no man ever loved.

130—"My mistress' eyes are nothing like the sun"

In this sonnet Shakespeare, himself influenced by the Petrarchan
conventions, pokes fun at them. It should be noted that it is the
convention, not the mistress, which is rejected, for the ironic tone
and mocking comparisons have often been misunderstood. "False
compare" is what the poet is protesting: the mistress' beauty, he
points out, is belied rather than praised by conventional, artificial,
and exaggerated comparisons. He is implying, as he does in many
of the sonnets, that love, which is strong enough to withstand
time and death, can accept reality and need not mock itself
with illusions.

My mistress' eyes are nothing like the sun,
Coral is far more red than her lips' red.
If snow be white, why then her breasts are dun,
If hairs be wires, black wires grow on her head.
I have seen roses damasked, red and white,
But no such roses see I in her cheeks.

And in some perfumes is there more delight
Than in the breath that from my mistress reeks.
I love to hear her speak, yet well I know
That music hath a far more pleasing sound.
I grant I never saw a goddess go,
My mistress, when she walks, treads on the ground.
    And yet, by Heaven, I think my love as rare
    As any she belied with false compare.

*At least two of Shakespeare's sonnets, 129 and 146, should be
compared with two of Sidney's. Lust, the "expense of spirit in a
waste of shame," is explored by Shakespeare in a series of violent
images that recall Sidney's "Thou blind man's mark. . . ." But
where Sidney affirms ultimate revulsion and rejects lust to embrace
virtue, Shakespeare's equal revulsion envisions no such outcome
of the long war between the opposed forces of man's dual nature:
"none knows well/To shun the heaven that leads men to this hell."
Like Sidney's "Leave me, O love . . . ," Shakespeare's "Poor soul
the centre of my sinful earth" contrasts the fading world of material
pleasures, which offers only "hours of dross," with the "terms
divine" for which it may be exchanged. But though theme, attitude,
and conclusion are identical, imagery and diction are startlingly
dissimilar. Sidney employs scriptural phrase and metaphor to
contrast the material and spiritual worlds in explicitly Christian
terms. Shakespeare presents the opposition in the concrete and
secular image of a civil war between the soul and the "rebel powers"
of sin. In place of Sidney's self-exhortation to follow the divine
light, he employs an intellectual argument: the folly of spending
substance upon the mortal body, the mere dwelling place of its
immortal tenant. And in place of Sidney's rhetorical farewell
to the world of dust and welcome to eternal love, Shakespeare ends
with a paradox that anticipates Donne's famous "Death, be not
proud . . .": death, which feeds on men, shall itself be consumed
and die while the soul lives forever.*

129–"Th' expense of spirit in a waste of shame"

Th' expense of spirit in a waste of shame
Is lust in action; and till action, lust
Is perjur'd, murd'rous, bloody, full of blame,
Savage, extreme, rude, cruel, not to trust;
Enjoy'd no sooner, but despisèd straight;
Past reason hunted; and no sooner had,
Past reason hated, as a swallow'd bait,
On purpose laid to make the taker mad;
Mad in pursuit, and in possession so;
Had, having, and in quest to have, extreme;
A bliss in proof, and prov'd, a very woe;
Before, a joy propos'd; behind, a dream.
    All this the world well knows; yet none knows well
    To shun the heaven that leads men to this hell.

146–"Poor soul, the centre of my sinful earth"

Poor soul, the centre of my sinful earth,
Fool'd by these rebel pow'rs that thee array,
Why dost thou pine within and suffer dearth,
Painting thy outward walls so costly gay?
Why so large cost, having so short a lease,
Dost thou upon thy fading mansion spend?
Shall worms, inheritors of this excess,
Eat up thy charge? Is this thy body's end?
Then, soul, live thou upon thy servant's loss,
And let that pine to aggravate thy store;
Buy terms divine in selling hours of dross;
Within be fed, without be rich no more:
    So shalt thou feed on Death that feeds on men,
    And Death once dead, there's no more dying then.

John Donne (*1572–1631*)

*Donne's "Holy Sonnets" are still unrivalled by any religious poetry
in their extraordinary mixture of qualities. Passionate and intense
to the verge of hysteria, they are also intellectual, witty, ingenious,
and paradoxical. New images drawn from science and theology
coexist with conventional figures adapted to new moods and new
uses. Love of God wrestles with terror of death and damnation;
piety at times is expressed in startling, almost blasphemous images;
and colloquial diction contrasts with sonorities of sound and
rhythm. Sin is the great theme in the poems, envisioned as a conflict
within man's heart, the battleground between God and the Devil.
The mood varies from fervent love to vivid fear to desperate hope
as the poet implores the grace and mercy of God. The "Holy
Sonnets" follow Wyatt in their adaptation of the Italian form of
the sonnet; the two quatrains rhyme a b b a a b a a, followed by a
sestet in which the rhyme scheme is varied but always ends with
a couplet.*

1–"Thou hast made me . . ."

*The dominant image is taken from science: the "iron heart," a
phrase that combines the literal and metaphorical force of "iron,"
is by its own sin drawn down toward hell, and the poet implores
God's grace to act as a more powerful magnet drawing it toward
heaven instead. Adamant is used in its now obsolete sense of a
lodestone possessing polarity.*

> Thou hast made me, And shall thy work decay?
> Repair me now, for now mine end doth haste,
> I run to death, and death meets me as fast,
> And all my pleasures are like yesterday,
> I dare not move my dim eyes any way,

Despair behind, and death before doth cast
Such terror, and my feebled flesh doth waste
By sin in it, which it t'wards hell doth weigh;
Only thou art above, and when towards thee
By thy leave I can look, I rise again;
But our old subtle foe so tempteth me,
That not one hour I can my self sustain;
Thy Grace may wing me to prevent his art
And thou like Adamant draw mine iron heart.

4–"At the round earth's imagined corners . . ."

*This sonnet is memorable equally for its breathtaking sweep of
vision from alpha to omega, from Creation to the Day of Judgment,
and for its splendors of sound. In the sestet the sonnet exhibits the
characteristic turn of mood of the Italian sonnet, as the poet's
vision shifts from past and future to his own present, the reality
of sin. It concludes with a paradox less flamboyant than that of 14,
but extraordinarily effective in the wit and force with which it uses
the doctrine of the Atonement: "Teach me how to repent; for
that's as good / As if thou hadst sealed my pardon with thy blood."
A more secular age than Donne's must perhaps be reminded that
there is no "as if" about this matter: Christ has sealed the
Christian's pardon with His blood, and all that is necessary for the
forgiveness of sin is repentance and the acceptance of His pardon.
Donne, at least, knows this and is, in effect, reminding the Savior
of it.*

At the round earth's imagined corners, blow
Your trumpets, angels; and arise, arise
From death, you numberless infinities
Of souls, and to your scattered bodies go;
All whom the flood did, and fire shall o'erthrow,
All whom war, dearth, age, agues, tyrannies,
Despair, law, chance hath slain, and you whose eyes
Shall behold God and never taste death's woe.
But let them sleep, Lord, and me mourn a space,
For if above all these my sins abound,

'Tis late to ask abundance of thy grace
When we are there; here on this lowly ground
Teach me how to repent; for that's as good
As if thou hadst sealed my pardon with thy blood.

10–"Death, be not proud . . ."

*The best-known of the "Holy Sonnets," remarkable for the
rallying mockery of its tone. The king of terrors is summarily told
to mind his manners and remember his place—which is, in effect,
nowhere—as the poem rises to exultation and triumph in its close:
"And death shall be no more; Death, thou shalt die." The mockery
is effectively and wittily delivered in a series of arguments—
arguments by analogy:*

From rest and sleep, which but thy pictures be,
Much pleasure; then from thee much more must flow,

arguments by syllogistic logic:

And soonest our best men with thee do go,
Rest of their bones, and soul's delivery.

arguments by example:

Thou art slave to fate, chance, kings, and desperate men,
And dost with poison, war, and sickness dwell:
And poppy or charms can make us sleep as well
And better than thy stroke;

Death, be not proud, though some have callèd thee
Mighty and dreadful, for thou art not so;
For those whom thou think'st thou dost overthrow
Die not, poor Death, nor yet canst thou kill me.
From rest and sleep, which but thy pictures be,
Much pleasure; then from thee much more must flow,
And soonest our best men with thee do go,
Rest of their bones, and soul's delivery.
Thou art slave to fate, chance, kings, and desperate men,
And dost with poison, war, and sickness dwell:

And poppy or charms can make us sleep as well
And better than thy stroke; why swell'st thou then?
One short sleep past, we wake eternally,
And death shall be no more; Death, thou shalt die.

13-"What if this present were the world's last
night?"

*The terrifying question with which this sonnet opens and the power
of its portrait of the crucified Christ tend to obscure the impact of
the central analogy. In his days of "idolatry" the poet had implored
his mistresses, in the best Petrarchan mode, to grant him sexual
love by using the argument that beauty implies and is a sign of
"pity." He now uses that same argument to implore Christ's love.*

What if this present were the world's last night?
Mark in my heart, O soul, where thou dost dwell,
The picture of Christ crucified, and tell
Whether his countenance can thee affright:
Tears in his eyes quench the amazing light,
Blood fills his frowns, which from his pierced head fell.
And can that tongue adjudge thee unto hell,
Which prayed forgiveness for his foes' fierce spite?
No, no; but as in my idolatry
I said to all my profane mistresses,
Beauty, of pity, foulness only is
A sign of rigor; so I say to thee:
To wicked spirits are horrid shapes assigned;
This beauteous form assumes a piteous mind.

14-"Batter my heart . . ."

*The analogy between sacred and profane love is repeated with
extraordinary force in 14. The sonnet opens with Donne's
characteristic active, almost violent diction and verbal paradox.
God is implored to act as the blacksmith of the soul, using his power
to "break, blow, burn, and make me new." The image now*

changes to a more conventional one. In a thousand Petrarchan
sonnets the mistress's or lover's heart had been compared to a
besieged town or fortress. Here, the soul is a tower besieged from
without by God. Within, however, it is subject to the power of sin,
which has captured Reason, God's viceroy or lieutenant. In a final
dramatic paradox the figure shifts again. God, the divine lover, is
implored to oust the devil to whom the soul is betrothed;
to free the soul by making it captive; and to make it chaste
by "ravishing" it Himself.

Batter my heart, three-personed God, for you
As yet but knock, breathe, shine, and seek to mend;
That I may rise and stand, o'erthrow me; and bend
Your force to break, blow, burn, and make me new.
I, like an usurped tower to another due,
Labor to admit you, but oh, to no end.
Reason, your viceroy in me, me should defend,
But is captived, and proves weak or untrue.
Yet dearly I love you, and would be lovèd fain,
But am betrothed unto your enemy;
Divorce me, untie or break that knot again;
Take me to you, imprison me, for I,
Except you enthrall me, never shall be free,
Nor ever chaste, except you ravish me.

George Herbert (1593–1633)

Redemption

Herbert, Donne's younger contemporary and friend, was much
influenced by the older poet. "Redemption" is ingenious and witty
in its condensation of the chief dogmas of Christianity—
Original Sin, the Incarnation, the Atonement—into the extended
metaphor of the tenant/landlord relationship.

Having been tenant long to a rich Lord,
  Not thriving, I resolvèd to be bold,
  And make a suit unto him to afford
A new small-rented lease and cancel th' old.
In heaven at his manor I him sought.
  They told me there that he was lately gone
  About some land which he had dearly bought
Long since on earth, to take possessïon.
I straight returned, and knowing his great birth,
  Sought him accordingly in great resorts,
  In cities, theaters, gardens, parks, and courts.
At length I heard a ragged noise and mirth
  Of thieves and murderers; there I him espied,
  Who straight, Your suit is granted, said, and died.

To His Mother

A protest against the Petrarchan fashion, pleading for religious themes in the lyric. In form, however, Herbert followed Surrey and Shakespeare rather than Donne.

My God, where is that ancient heat towards thee
  Wherewith whole shoals of martyrs once did burn,
  Besides their other flames? Doth poetry
Wear Venus' livery, only serve her turn?
Why are not sonnets made of thee, and lays
  Upon thine altar burnt? Cannot thy love
  Heighten a spirit to sound out thy praise
As well as any she? Cannot thy dove
Outstrip their Cupid easily in flight?
  Or, since thy ways are deep and still the same,
  Will not a verse run smooth that bears thy name?
Why doth that fire, which by thy power and might
  Each breast does feel, no braver fuel choose
  Than that which one day worms may chance refuse?

John Milton (1608–1674)

*However different in subject matter and tone, Milton's sonnets
resemble one another in their characteristic mixture of the personal
with the impersonal; the noble egoism with which a great poet
expresses his sense of his own identity, mission, and hope of fame;
their imagery drawn from classical, biblical, and doctrinal sources;
their invocation of lofty political and religious principles; their
rich, full-voweled diction; and their complex but logical and clear
grammatical structure. Some, like 7, 8, and 23, are intensely personal.
These include the poet's sense of his vocation, belief in future
recognition, and submission to his "great task-Master"; the half-
playful, half-earnest summons to the soldiery to spare his house on
the grounds that he can make them famous, and the wholly earnest
comparison of himself with the august poets of ancient Greece;
his feelings on his blindness; and those for his dead wife. The last
poem is almost intolerably moving in its close, where we are
reminded all at once of his irremediable loss and the fact that the
blind poet has seen his wife's face only in dreams.*

7–On His Being Arrived to the Age of Twenty-three

How soon hath Time, the subtle thief of youth,
   Stolen on his wing my three and twentieth year!
   My hasting days fly on with full career,
   But my late spring no bud or blossom shew'th.
Perhaps my semblance might deceive the truth,
   That I to manhood am arrived so near,
   And inward ripeness doth much less appear,
   That some more timely-happy spirits indu'th.
Yet be it less or more, or soon or slow,
   It shall be still in strictest measure even

To that same lot, however mean or high,
Toward which Time leads me, and the will of Heaven.
All is, if I have grace to use it so,
As ever in my great Task-master's eye.

8–When the Assault Was Intended to the City

Captain, or colonel, or knight in arms,
Whose chance on these defenceless doors may seize,
If deed of honour did thee ever please,
Guard them, and him within protect from harms.
He can requite thee, for he knows the charms
That call fame on such gentle acts as these,
And he can spread thy name o'er lands and seas,
Whatever clime the sun's bright circle warms.
Lift not thy spear against the Muse's bower;
The great Emathian conqueror bid spare
The house of Pindarus, when temple and tower
Went to the ground; and the repeated air
Of sad Electra's Poet had the power
To save the Athenian walls from ruin bare.

12–"I did but prompt the age . . ."

Milton's answer to the protests that followed his publication of
Tetrachordon, *a pamphlet in which he had argued for scriptural
warrant for divorce. The sonnet is a masterpiece of compression and
condensation. Beginning with a line in his own defense, he turns
on his attackers with invective that is both savage in mood and
precise in thought: the owl, according to Pliny, is an emblem of
darkness; the cuckoo of ingratitude; the dog of quarrelsomeness
and detraction; and asses and apes speak for themselves. Immediately
the poet elevates the mood with figures from classical mythology
and Scripture and then—as he did at length in such prose works as*
The Tenure of Kings and Magistrates—*defines true liberty as
distinct from license and associates it with wisdom and virtue.*

I did but prompt the age to quit their clogs
  By the known rules of ancient liberty,
  When straight a barbarous noise environs me
  Of owls and cuckoos, asses, apes, and dogs;
As when those hinds that were transformed to frogs
  Railed at Latona's twin-born progeny,
  Which after held the Sun and Moon in fee.
  But this is got by casting pearl to hogs,
That bawl for freedom in their senseless mood,
  And still revolt when Truth would set them free.
  Licence they mean when they cry Liberty;
For who loves that must first be wise and good:
  But from that mark how far they rove we see,
  For all this waste of wealth and loss of blood.

14–On the Religious Memory of Mrs. Catharine Thomson

*This sonnet is like a morality play: Faith and Love summon the
soul to heaven, to which it is followed by works and alms, which
"Stayed not behind, nor in the grave were trod," as in the famous*
Everyman. *Milton thus resolves the long-standing and much-debated
controversy among Protestants as to whether redemption depends
on faith or on works, declaring the necessity for and the
operation of both in a good life. Like the earlier* Lycidas, *the
conclusion of the poem shows the departed enjoying
the "pure immortal streams" of heaven.*

When Faith and Love, which parted from thee never,
  Had ripened thy just soul to dwell with God,
  Meekly thou didst resign this earthy load
  Of death, called life, which us from life doth sever.
Thy works, and alms, and all thy good endeavour,
  Stayed not behind, nor in the grave were trod;
  But, as Faith pointed with her golden rod,
  Followed thee up to joy and bliss for ever.
Love led them on; and Faith, who knew them best

Thy handmaids, clad them o'er with purple beams
  And azure wings, that up they flew so drest,
And speak the truth of thee on glorious themes
  Before the Judge; who thenceforth bid thee rest,
  And drink thy fill of pure immortal streams.

15–On the Lord General Fairfax

*The sonnet to Fairfax, remarkable for the magnificent cadenced and
voweled roll of its opening quatrain, modulates first into restrained
invective against political opponents; then to comment, both
lofty and indignant, on politicians of Milton's own party; and
concludes with a call to peaceful tasks of civic virtue.*

Fairfax, whose name in arms through Europe rings,
  Filling each mouth with envy or with praise,
  And all her jealous monarchs with amaze,
  And rumours loud that daunt remotest kings,
Thy firm unshaken virtue ever brings
  Victory home, though new rebellions raise
  Their Hydra heads, and the false North displays
  Her broken league to imp their serpent wings.
O yet a nobler task awaits thy hand
  (For what can war but endless war still breed?)
  Till truth and right from violence be freed,
And public faith cleared from the shameful brand
  Of public fraud. In vain doth Valour bleed,
  While Avarice and Rapine share the land.

18–On the Late Massacre in Piedmont

*Milton's greatest sonnet—some say the greatest ever written in
English[7]—is by all odds the poem on the Piedmont massacre. Here
the Protestant poet, contemplating the murder of Protestants by
Catholic forces, suits sound and cadence to occasion and mood*

---

[7] Frank Allen Patterson, *The Student's Milton* (New York, 1930), p. 54 of the
Notes.

by drawing the long vowels out from word to word and line
to line in a prolonged moan of pity for the victims and indignation
against Rome, the "triple Tyrant."

Avenge, O Lord, thy slaughtered Saints, whose bones
  Lie scattered on the Alpine mountains cold;
  Even them who kept thy truth so pure of old,
When all our fathers worshiped stocks and stones,
Forget not: in thy book record their groans
  Who were thy sheep, and in their ancient fold
  Slain by the bloody Piemontese, that rolled
Mother with infant down the rocks. Their moans
The vales redoubled to the hills, and they
  To heaven. Their martyred blood and ashes sow
O'er all the Italian fields, where still doth sway
The triple Tyrant; that from these may grow
A hundredfold, who, having learnt thy way,
  Early may fly the Babylonian woe.

23–On His Deceased Wife

Methought I saw my late espousèd saint
  Brought to me like Alcestis from the grave,
  Whom Jove's great son to her glad husband gave,
  Rescued from Death by force, though pale and faint.
Mine, as whom washed from spot of child-bed taint
  Purification in the Old Law did save,
  And such as yet once more I trust to have
  Full sight of her in Heaven without restraint,
Came vested all in white, pure as her mind.
  Her face was veiled; yet to my fancied sight
  Love, sweetness, goodness, in her person shined
So clear as in no face with more delight.
  But, oh! as to embrace me she inclined,
  I waked, she fled, and day brought back my night.

The Eighteenth Century

The eighteenth century was an age of great satire and of a variety of meditative, reflective, and descriptive verse. The Augustan poets, for the most part, cultivated couplets—octosyllabic or heroic —and blank verse as forms more suited to their purposes than the narrow and highly structured confines of the sonnet. Their lyric form was the ode, of which Dryden, Gray, and Collins, to name only three, produced fine examples. Neglected thus by the great poets of the time, the sonnet suffered even more from the attention of inferior poets. In the latter part of the century, largely under the influence of Thomas Warton—greater as a man of letters than as a poet—a multitude of commonplace and popular writers produced a multitude of bad sonnets. These appeared mostly in the magazines of the day and can now, happily, be forgotten.

It is not remarkable, then, that between the death of Milton and the youth of Wordsworth, a period of more than a century and a quarter, so few good sonnets were produced. The three lone sonnets that stand here are not so much representatives of their time as reminders that the sonnet survived even this drear and waste period of its history. None of the poems is first-rate. All are competent and respectable examples of the form and interesting as well for the glimpses they afford of the ways the sonnet was accommodating itself to the sensibility of the age.

All three show the strain of philosophic melancholy that was developing in the meditative poetry of the time, of which Edward Young's long poem, "Night Thoughts on Life, Death, and Immortality," and Robert Blair's "The Grave" are typical examples. It is a strain seldom heard in the Renaissance sonnet. Pride, passion, irony, grim warning, even—in Donne's case—terror and despair; but not this gentle and resigned sadness. It reminds us that this was the age of Wesley and of Methodism (whose poetic spokesman Cowper was) and of a widespread dissatisfaction with the cool, rational religion of the deists and the now arid and sterile formulas and class-bound practices of the Church of England. "To Mrs. Unwin" and "December Morning," like the hymns of Charles

Wesley and Isaac Watts, reveal the new emotional power of a revitalized Christianity in which deeds and the personal relationship of the soul to God are more important than institution and creed. "Thus," says a distinguished critic,[1] "the Age of Reason modulated gradually into the Age of Sensibility."

Also audible in all three poems is a more personal and individual note than had hitherto been characteristic of the sonnet. Gray's grief for his friend, however controlled by convention and diction, is a personal emotion, far more poignant in its sense of actual loss than anything that had preceded it in the sonnet form. The poet is not indulging in an exercise of intellect or of emotion for its own sake, as the Renaissance sonneteers too often were, but is expressing a felt sorrow. So, too, Cowper's praise of Mrs. Unwin has a more personal ring than Milton's "On the Religious Memory of Mrs. Catharine Thomson." New also are Mrs. Seward's moral reflections on the human situation. All have a directness of statement, a comparative freedom from symbol and image, and from metaphysical poetry's delight in word play and intellectual games. In their expression of genuine feeling, in a new simplicity of image, diction, and syntax, in a softened sensibility responsive to experience and emotion, they are precursors of the new age that was to begin with Wordsworth.

Thomas Gray (1716–1771)

On the Death of Mr. Richard West

An interesting and successful mixture of the personal and the conventional. The diction is artificial and stylized in typical eighteenth-century fashion—redd'ning Phoebus, amorous descant, busy race—*and the conventions are neoclassical: nature is still beautiful, but I cannot feel its beauty. It is the pull against these of*

[1] David Daiches, *A Critical History of English Literature* (New York, 1960), II, 661.

the low-keyed, controlled emotion, reinforced by repetition and
regularity of rhyme scheme, that makes the poem.

> In vain to me the smiling Mornings shine,
> And redd'ning Phoebus lifts his golden fire;
> The birds in vain their amorous descant join;
> Or cheerful fields resume their green attire;
> These ears, alas! for other notes repine,
> A different object do these eyes require.
> My lonely anguish melts no heart but mine;
> And in my breast the imperfect joys expire.
> Yet Morning smiles the busy race to cheer,
> And new-born pleasure brings to happier men;
> The fields to all their wonted tribute bear;
> To warm their little loves the birds complain:
> I fruitless mourn to him, that cannot hear,
> And weep the more, because I weep in vain.

William Cowper (1731–1800)

To Mrs. Unwin

This sonnet should be compared with Milton's "On the Religious
Memory of Mrs. Catharine Thomson" (p. 59). Cowper's poem is
softer, more personal in both feeling and diction, and less precise
and intellectual in its use of the conventional symbols and images
or in any such play on words as Milton makes: "this earthy load/Of
Death, call'd Life; which us from Life doth sever." The whole
moves on a more human, a less lofty and abstract level. Milton
makes us believe in Mrs. Thomson in heaven; Cowper
makes us believe in Mrs. Unwin on earth.

> Mary! I want a lyre with other strings,
> Such aid from heaven as some have feigned they drew,
> An eloquence scarce given to mortals, new
> And undebased by praise of meaner things;

That, ere through age or woe I shed my wings,
I may record thy worth with honour due,
In verse as musical as thou art true,
And that immortalizes whom it sings.
But thou hast little need. There is a Book
By seraphs writ with beams of heavenly light,
On which the eyes of God not rarely look,
A chronicle of actions just and bright;—
There all thy deeds, my faithful Mary, shine;
And since thou own'st that praise, I spare thee mine.

Anna Seward (1747–1809)

December Morning

*The sonnet combines typical eighteenth-century diction and
abstractions, like Wisdom and the Muse, with a wealth of realistic
observed detail. Its pious reflection, reinforced by relentless
conventional adjectives, sounds the typical note of the
earnest Victorian Age to follow.*

I love to rise ere gleams the tardy light,
Winter's pale dawn; and as warm fires illume,
And cheerful tapers shine around the room,
Through misty windows bend my musing sight,
Where, round the dusky lawn, the mansions white,
With shutters closed, peer faintly through the gloom
That slow recedes; while yon grey spires assume,
Rising from their dark pile, an added height
By indistinctness given.—Then to decree
The grateful thoughts to God, ere they unfold
To friendship or the Muse, or seek with glee
Wisdom's rich page. O hours more worth than gold,
By whose blest use we lengthen life, and, free
From drear decays of age, outlive the old!

The Romantic Period

When, on an afternoon in 1801, Dorothy Wordsworth read her brother the sonnets of Milton, the sonnet form reassumed an old inheritance and entered upon a new destiny. Wordsworth was to restore its place in English poetry more effectually than Milton himself had done. For after Milton had come the long period of the sonnet's disuse by gifted poets, while after Wordsworth came Keats, the Rossettis, and—looming in the distance—Gerard Manley Hopkins, and after him a host of talented and experimental practitioners of this form.

Not all of Wordsworth's sonnets, by any means, are great, nor even good. He wrote far too many—more than five hundred—as he wrote too much poetry altogether during his long life. But a handful of distinguished sonnets are among his best poems.

> The sonnet, in its freedom of choice in theme and emotion, united to its exacting discipline, and to its special need of a clear intellectual basis and articulation, was a predestined form for Wordsworth. He was drawn to this form because of its capacities for prophetic, uplifted, and indignant utterance.[1]

That is to say, Wordsworth's sonnets reveal in brief compass, in substance and structure, in theme and mood the peculiar and individual qualities of his temperament and of his genius.

In form, he turned to Milton and to the Italian sonnet as Milton had practiced it. Only one of Wordsworth's sonnets is in the Shakespearean pattern. The rest follow the traditional Italian measures or exhibit varieties of that basic structure invented by himself. Unlike Milton, Wordsworth wrote not only separate sonnets; in *The River Duddon* and *Ecclesiastical Sonnets* he revived the sonnet sequence after two hundred years of disuse. With one or two exceptions, however, the sonnets of these sequences are not among his most successful.

Again like Milton, Wordsworth avoided romantic or sensual love

[1] Oliver Elton, *A Survey of English Literature*, 1780–1880 (New York, 1920), II, 81.

as a theme. His characteristic subject matter is some item of his personal experience, but never that experience which, to the Elizabethan sonneteers, had been the be-all and end-all. He records his responses to places, times, actions, events, books, paintings, ideas, political figures, friends, family. Each sonnet tends to be a brief verse essay on some topic to which he responds with deep feeling; for despite his avoidance of erotic love, he regarded the sonnet as particularly suited to the expression of personal emotion. Almost never, however, does Wordsworth explore and express emotion for its own sake. Rather, the emotion he feels becomes a kind of spiritual conductor leading him from the visible into the invisible world.

In this, as in many other respects, Wordsworth's sonnets are a part of the history of the romantic movement, as the sonnet itself is a part of the history of lyric poetry. *Romanticism* and the "romantic movement" are, of course, bushel-basket terms, mere shorthand for a wide variety of features thus lumped together, though occurring in separate and often very dissimilar works. Central to the meaning of *romantic,* however, is the importance attached to the individual self, its feeling and experience, and its efforts to discover through the imagination some transcendental reality reflected in the world of nature. The romantic poets display the world of nature acting upon the imagination in such a way as to set visionary powers in action and to reveal the truth and reality of the unseen world.

The romantic sense of the bond between the self, nature, and reality explains a seeming, not a real paradox: Wordsworth's sonnets, despite their exploitation of his own experience, are not really personal; they are *subjective.* Unlike many of Milton's and most nineteenth-century sonnets, Wordsworth's tend always to place the poet's emotion and experience within a far broader, more abstract and impersonal frame of reference. Through the inner world, as he experiences and responds to the world around him, the poet becomes aware of, and gives utterance to, insights into man's nature and the nature of the universe itself. Wordsworth's typical subject matter, thus, is some aspect of the relation between himself as man, nature, and spiritual truth. His mood and tone vary: now exalted with a sense of the awe and mystery of things; now impassioned and indignant; now soft and more familiar as he speaks of human love and human grief. Always, however, the poet is grave and lofty, his voice that of the seer and prophet rather than the singer. His sonnets are marked by a simplicity of diction and of syntax that matches their clarity of thought and their precise structure. His imagery is never merely ornamental or arbitrary but always integral to form and substance.

Though Wordsworth's sonnets do not display the range, the learning, and the intellectual quality of Milton's, nor the sensuous richness and passion of Keats', a few of them are among the greatest written in English. They are wonderfully fresh in perception, full of feeling and sympathy; theme, sound, diction, image, and tone work together to achieve one effect, one mood. The best give that sense that only great poets manage to convey (and even they, rarely) of the imagination penetrating the phenomenal world to a reality beyond appearances.

Wordsworth's contribution to the evolution of the sonnet form was as great as or even greater than Milton's. He ratified the freedom that Milton had established from the traditional characteristics of the Elizabethans; and he freed the sonnet from the sentimentality, melancholy, and above all the triviality, of the eighteenth century. His two great romantic contemporaries, Blake and Coleridge, were not sonneteers. The latter produced a few second-rate sonnets, but none compare in quality with Wordsworth's great poems. It was not until nearly a generation after that memorable afternoon in 1801 that Keats, the youngest member of a second group of romantic poets including Byron and Shelley, in a scant half-dozen sonnets— compared to the hundreds Wordsworth produced—rivalled the achievements of the older poet and those of Milton himself.

The major influence on Keats' sonnets was Leigh Hunt, though it was an influence Keats rapidly outgrew. His conception of the sonnet form, for the most part, was likewise that held by Hunt, though in practice Keats was more flexible. Hunt set forth his views in "An Essay on the Cultivation, History, and Varieties of the Species of Poem Called the Sonnet," written as an introductory section of the anthology *The Book of the Sonnet,* which he published in collaboration with S. Adams Lee. In this essay Hunt voiced a strong preference for the strict Italian form, with two rhymes in the octave and never more than three in the sestet. He stigmatized the English, or Shakespearean, form as "illegitimate," though he did go so far as to say that the sonnets of Shakespeare "conquer all objection." It is to be hoped he had the same opinion of Keats' "Bright star . . . ," in which the younger poet, too, demonstrated the perfection of which that illegitimate form is capable. Hunt himself practiced the sonnet form not without distinction. The compactness and the discipline it demands in both form and thought lent him the artistic control his longer poems lack. He was, however, inescapably a minor poet whose chief interest today lies in the young Keats' brief discipleship.

Because of the brevity of his life and the confining circumstances of poverty and ill-health, Keats' stature as a poet is exhibited to the full in a mere handful of poems, notably the great odes and a few sonnets. Where his poetry fails, it does so through vagueness and diffuseness of structure, overly lush and sweet diction, and forced or inappropriate imagery. Conversely, where it succeeds, it does so by intensity, concentration, and a richness both sensuous and symbolic. "Load every rift with ore," he advised the sometimes even more vague and diffuse Shelley; and he tried increasingly to follow this advice himself. In his best sonnets, as in the odes, he succeeded. Senses, mind, and imagination work together through structure, symbol, and language to produce brief and perfect poems, uniting qualities found before only in those of Shakespeare. The sonnet form disciplined Keats' tendency to diffuse and dreamy vagueness and forced him to tighter structure, harder thought, more concentrated imagery, and more sinewy and athletic diction. It was a mold into which he could pour his intensity of feeling and sensuous response to nature, to beauty, to love, his aching awareness of mortality, his love of poetry, and hope of fame. These are the subjects of his sonnets. At their best, they show the imagination of a great poet penetrating the seen and the unseen world and shaping insight and feeling into form as perfect as that of the Grecian urn.

Wordsworth and Keats between them share the honors of the romantic sonnet. Of the two, Keats proved to be a greater and more permanent influence on the poets of the Victorian Age. That he was not always a good influence was inevitable. His successors found it easier to imitate his bad qualities—the cloying sweetness, the soft, lush diction and cadence, the vague, youthful dreaminess—than the packed richness, the luminous imagination, the passion of his best verse. So pervasive, in fact, became the influence not of Keats himself but of a host of "Keatsians" that in the twentieth century strong and original talents have had to fight free of this legacy before they were able to write their own poetry.

William Wordsworth (1770–1850)

"Nuns fret not at their convent's narrow room"

Nuns fret not at their convent's narrow room;
And hermits are contented with their cells;
And students with their pensive citadels;
Maids at the wheel, the weaver at his loom,
Sit blithe and happy; bees that soar for bloom,
High as the highest Peak of Furness-fells,
Will murmur by the hour in foxglove bells:
In truth the prison, unto which we doom
Ourselves, no prison is: and hence for me,
In sundry moods, 'twas pastime to be bound
Within the Sonnet's scanty plot of ground;
Pleased if some Souls (for such there needs must be)
Who have felt the weight of too much liberty,
Should find brief solace there, as I have found.

Composed upon Westminster Bridge

*Remarkable for the way in which it combines scene and mood.
The city, at a moment in early morning when it is most unlike itself
and most like nature, is described in such a way as to unite the
sight itself and the poet's response to the sight. Beginning with
emphatic but general statements that are a prelude to the real subject
of the poem, Wordsworth, in the fourth line, gives an image of
the city as a living creature wearing a beauty that is of nature,
not man. Silent and bare, adjectives least like the common attributes
of a city, are followed by a particular catalogue of urban imagery;
but the difference of the scene from one of normal urban activity*

*is underlined by the conclusion of the octave. That the city has,
for the moment, been transfigured into the world of nature is
reiterated by the next two lines; and the picture of the hushed calm
of early morning is followed by the rapt exclamation "Dear God!"
in which the poet registers his own sense of awe and utter peace.
The images of the last two lines reinforce the suggestion of a living
creature, of a beauty and tranquillity commonly found in nature,
not in ordinary urban life. The whole poem vividly presents a
moment of imaginative vision in which a great city is seen and
experienced as part of the natural world.*

> Earth has not anything to show more fair:
> Dull would he be of soul who could pass by
> A sight so touching in its majesty:
> This City now doth, like a garment, wear
> The beauty of the morning; silent, bare,
> Ships, towers, domes, theatres, and temples lie
> Open unto the fields, and to the sky;
> All bright and glittering in the smokeless air.
> Never did sun more beautifully steep
> In his first splendour, valley, rock, or hill;
> Ne'er saw I, never felt, a calm so deep!
> The river glideth at his own sweet will:
> Dear God! The very houses seem asleep;
> And all that mighty heart is lying still!

"It is a beauteous evening . . ."

*Note the religious imagery of the octave, in which the evening
is described as filled with, and responsive to, a divine spirit.
All the terms of the first five lines—calm, free, holy, Nun,
Breathless, adoration, tranquillity, gentleness, broods"—suggest the
silence and communion of worship and nature as the worshipper
of God immanent in it. The last three lines of the octave introduce,
and in their sound and cadence imitate, the eternal movement and
sound of the sea—a contrast with the utter calm of the evening but
also the dwelling place of "the mighty Being." In the sestet, the
poet turns from God in nature to God in the child: the grown man*

experiences God through nature, but the child intuitively and directly. Solemn, divine, *and* worshipp'st *link sestet with octave and support the idea that the child experiences and worships God directly, like nature and not through nature.*

It is a beauteous evening, calm and free,
The holy time is quiet as a Nun
Breathless with adoration; the broad sun
Is sinking down in its tranquillity;
The gentleness of heaven broods o'er the Sea:
Listen! the mighty Being is awake,
And doth with his eternal motion make
A sound like thunder—everlastingly.
Dear Child! dear Girl! that walkest with me here,
If thou appear untouched by solemn thought,
Thy nature is not therefore less divine:
Thou liest in Abraham's bosom all the year;
And worshipp'st at the Temple's inner shrine,
God being with thee when we know it not.

To Toussaint L'Ouverture

Again an example of Wordsworth's tendency to generalize. The fate of the Haitian leader brings the poet in the sestet to the consolation that, in some way, the powers and sublime experiences of the human spirit are a part of the larger powers of the universe itself. This sense of a mysterious bond between man, nature, and some transcendental reality breathing through nature is Wordsworth's hallmark.

Toussaint, the most unhappy man of men!
Whether the whistling Rustic tend his plough
Within thy hearing, or thy head be now
Pillowed in some deep dungeon's earless den;—
O miserable Chieftain! where and when
Wilt thou find patience! Yet die not; do thou
Wear rather in thy bonds a cheerful brow:
Though fallen thyself, never to rise again,

Live, and take comfort. Thou hast left behind
Powers that will work for thee; air, earth, and skies;
There's not a breathing of the common wind
That will forget thee; thou hast great allies;
Thy friends are exultations, agonies,
And love, and man's unconquerable mind.

On the Extinction of the Venetian Republic

*Another illustration of Wordsworth's tendency always to refer
particulars of time, place, or experience to some general idea or
principle. The greatness and significance of the Venetian Republic
are presented in a series of metaphors that turn on the analogy
of human life and human greatness. The analogy not only makes
the republic itself more vivid, but the general conclusion of the last
two lines more emphatic and convincing. The poem becomes
more than just a memorial to the past greatness of Venice; it is a
lament for the transitoriness of human glory and a celebration
nevertheless of the spirit of man.*

Once did she hold the gorgeous east in fee;
And was the safeguard of the west: the worth
Of Venice did not fall below her birth,
Venice, the eldest Child of Liberty.
She was a maiden City, bright and free;
No guile seduced, no force could violate;
And, when she took unto herself a Mate,
She must espouse the everlasting Sea.
And what if she had seen those glories fade,
Those titles vanish, and that strength decay;
Yet shall some tribute of regret be paid
When her long life hath reached its final day:
Men are we, and must grieve when even the Shade
Of that which once was great, is passed away.

London, 1802

Milton! thou shouldst be living at this hour:
England hath need of thee: she is a fen
Of stagnant waters: altar, sword, and pen,
Fireside, the heroic wealth of hall and bower,
Have forfeited their ancient English dower
Of inward happiness. We are selfish men;
Oh! raise us up, return to us again;
And give us manners, virtue, freedom, power.
Thy soul was like a Star, and dwelt apart;
Thou hadst a voice whose sound was like the sea:
Pure as the naked heavens, majestic, free,
So didst thou travel on life's common way,
In cheerful godliness; and yet thy heart
The lowliest duties on herself did lay.

"It is not to be thought of . . ."

*A fine example of Wordsworth's most sonorous manner and vatic
mood. Note the handling of the vowels: round, open o's and u's
alternate and harmonize with long a's and e's; the whole sonnet
seems to be spoken in one deep breath. Syntax reinforces sound:
in this otherwise regular Italian sonnet, Wordsworth avoids the
sharp break at the end of the octave and instead runs the single long
sentence of the octave over to the middle of the ninth line. The
last four lines also are enjambed like the first nine, with only one
line in the sonnet end-stopped. The structure thus contributes, like
the sound, to the effect of a single sustained utterance.*

It is not to be thought of that the Flood
Of British freedom, which, to the open sea
Of the world's praise, from dark antiquity
Hath flowed, "with pomp of waters, unwithstood,"
Roused though it be full often to a mood
Which spurns the check of salutary bands,

That this most famous Stream in bogs and sands
Should perish; and to evil and to good
Be lost for ever. In our halls is hung
Armoury of the invincible Knights of old:
We must be free or die, who speak the tongue
That Shakespeare spake; the faith and morals hold
Which Milton held.—In every thing we are sprung
Of Earth's first blood, have titles manifold.

"The world is too much with us . . ."

Compare with the sonnet "Composed Upon Westminster Bridge."
Here, Wordsworth laments the alienation in modern, urban,
industrial society of man from nature. In the ancient world
man lived in harmony with nature and perceived it as filled with
divinity. Modern man, immersed in "getting and spending," is
oblivious to his own kinship with nature and to the spirit that
breathes through it. The imagery of lines 5–7 is extraordinary in the
vividness and immediacy with which it conveys various aspects of
the natural world: beauty, sensuality, violence, and fragility.
Note the long, drawn-out cadence and mouth-filling vowels of the
last line.

The world is too much with us; late and soon,
Getting and spending, we lay waste our powers:
Little we see in Nature that is ours;
We have given our hearts away, a sordid boon!
This Sea that bares her bosom to the moon;
The winds that will be howling at all hours,
And are up-gathered now like sleeping flowers;
For this, for everything, we are out of tune;
It moves us not.—Great God! I'd rather be
A Pagan suckled in a creed outworn;
So might I, standing on this pleasant lea,
Have glimpses that would make me less forlorn;
Have sight of Proteus rising from the sea;
Or hear old Triton blow his wreathèd horn.

"Surprised by joy . . ."

*This sonnet, prompted by the poet's memory of his dead daughter
Catharine, is a good example of his own definition of poetry as
"emotion recollected in tranquillity." The mood of the present,
in which joy has taken him suddenly off guard, mingles with
his recollection of past loss and anticipation of never-ending sorrow
to make a single piercing statement about love, grief, and life itself.*

Surprised by joy—impatient as the Wind
I turned to share the transport—Oh! with whom
But Thee, deep buried in the silent tomb,
That spot which no vicissitude can find?
Love, faithful love, recalled thee to my mind—
But how could I forget thee? Through what power,
Even for the least division of an hour,
Have I been so beguiled as to be blind
To my most grievous loss!—That thought's return
Was the worst pang that sorrow ever bore,
Save one, one only, when I stood forlorn,
Knowing my heart's best treasure was no more;
That neither present time, nor years unborn
Could to my sight that heavenly face restore.

After-Thought

*Here again, as in the sonnet on Toussaint L'Ouverture, the present
scene evokes in the poet a vision, an intuitive knowledge of a
transcendent meaning and value to human life, a sense that virtuous
men are in tune with the unheard but felt harmonies of a spiritual
world. Note that the "exultations" and "agonies" of the earlier
poem have in the later one become the Christian graces of faith,
hope, and charity.*

I thought of Thee, my partner and my guide,
As being past away.—Vain sympathies!

For, backward, Duddon! as I cast my eyes,
I see what was, and is, and will abide:
Still glides the Stream, and shall for ever glide:
The Form remains, the Function never dies;
While we, the brave, the mighty, and the wise,
We Men, who in our morn of youth defied
The elements, must vanish:—be it so!
Enough, if something from our hands have power
To live, and act, and serve the future hour;
And if, as toward the silent tomb we go,
Through love, through hope, and faith's transcendent dower,
We feel that we are greater than we know.

Mutability

*The best of the "Ecclesiastical Sonnets" series and one of the finest
sonnets ever written. In thought, it repeats Wordsworth's theme
of the link between man's nature and the unseen realities of the
universe: the virtuous man is attuned to the "musical but
melancholy chime" of mutability, the constant condition of all
nature. The imagery is less concrete than that of the earlier sonnets;
indeed, it functions more as symbol than image. The dissolution
of all the apparently solid forms of things is presented first in terms
of nature, then the works of man, and finally by implication man
himself. The tower's "crown of weeds," particularly, is a marvelously
effective and ironic symbol of the brief, fragile, and essentially trivial
nature of man's works and of his long history.*

*Sound and structure buttress substance and mood. The "melting"
quality of the apparently durable forms of the world is conveyed
by soft and fluid liquids, sibilants, and nasals; and the tower's
sudden collapse, suggested by* shout, *is emphatic both in sound and
placement. Though the sonnet is in the conventional Italian form,
the shift in subject comes not at the end of the octave but at the
beginning of the seventh line, and is signalled by the third rhyme
sound of* care, *at the end of the sixth line. The rhymes of the sestet
lead back into those of the octave, bringing the end back to the
beginning in a kind of circular movement. Abstract as it is in both
subject and imagery, the poem is lent more concreteness and unity*

through its rhyme scheme and sound devices. The last line,
especially, is one of those rare and unforgettable utterances that echo
in the mind forever. The whole poem moves on a level of grandeur
and universality seldom equalled.

From low to high doth dissolution climb,
And sink from high to low, along a scale
Of awful notes, whose concord shall not fail;
A musical but melancholy chime,
Which they can hear who meddle not with crime,
Nor avarice, nor over-anxious care.
Truth fails not; but her outward forms that bear
The longest date do melt like frosty rime,
That in the morning whitened hill and plain
And is no more; drop like the tower sublime
Of yesterday, which royally did wear
His crown of weeds, but could not even sustain
Some casual shout that broke the silent air,
Or the unimaginable touch of Time.

Blanco White (1775–1841)

To Night

This sonnet was praised by Coleridge as the finest in the language.
The nineteenth century unquestionably had more of an appetite
for rhetoric and for detecting moral and religious analogies in the
natural world than does the twentieth. Nevertheless, the sonnet is,
in its own way, impressive. It is made up of neat antitheses and
analogies, of a whole series of terms that balance, contrast, and
interweave: night and day, darkness and light, death and life, the
world below and the starry heavens above, appearance and reality.
Night and darkness, analogues of death, nevertheless reveal the
stars that have been concealed by the blaze of the sun men associate
with life. So death, which they dread as the end of life and light,

may reveal unseen and glorious realities. Though the subject is a
romantic one, in structure and diction the poem harks back to the
formality, the classical taste for balance, parallelism, and logic,
and the vocabulary of the Age of Reason. The form, like Wyatt's,
is hybrid—the Italian sonnet with a closing couplet.

Mysterious Night! when our first parent knew
   Thee from report divine, and heard thy name,
   Did he not tremble for this lovely frame,
This glorious canopy of light and blue?
Yet 'neath a curtain of translucent dew,
   Bathed in the rays of the great setting flame,
   Hesperus with the host of heaven came,
And lo! Creation widened in man's view.

Who could have thought such darkness lay concealed
Within thy beams, O Sun! or who could find,
   Whilst flow'r and leaf and insect stood revealed,
That to such countless orbs thou mad'st us blind!
   Why do we then shun Death with anxious strife?
   If Light can thus deceive, wherefore not Life?

James Leigh Hunt (1784–1859)

To the Grasshopper and the Cricket

This sonnet should be compared with Keats' on the same subject
(p. 85). Hunt's has a tender charm, an intimate sense of familiarity
with nature, and a straightforward simplicity of language.
Compared to Keats' sonnet, however, it moves on a lower level.
It is expository where Keats is lyrical, pedestrian and moralistic
where Keats is sensuous and imaginative.

Green little vaulter in the sunny grass,
   Catching your heart up at the feel of June,

Sole voice that's heard amidst the lazy noon,
When ev'n the bees lag at the summoning brass;—
And you, warm little housekeeper, who class
 With those who think the candles come too soon,
 Loving the fire, and with your tricksome tune
Nick the glad silent moments as they pass;—

Oh sweet and tiny cousins, that belong,
 One to the fields, the other to the hearth,
Both have your sunshine; both, though small, are strong
 At your clear hearts; and both were sent on earth
To sing in thoughtful ears this natural song—
 In doors and out,—summer and winter,—Mirth.

To a Fish

Humor in the sonnet was virtually unknown. Sir John Davies'
so-called "Gulling Sonnets," and Shakespeare's "My mistress's
eyes are nothing like the sun," attacks on the outworn sonnet
conventions of their day, are rare instances. Sonneteers have tended
to take both themselves and the form seriously; in fact, an excess
of seriousness, inflated to grandiloquence and pomposity, plus the
sentimentality that so often accompanies it, has generally been the
curse of the inferior sonnet. Hunt's playful treatments of
irreconcilable differences in viewpoint are thus a welcome change,
though of no great merit poetically.

You strange, astonished-looking, angle-faced,
 Dreary-mouthed, gaping wretches of the sea,
 Gulping salt-water everlastingly,
Cold-blooded, though with red your blood be graced,
And mute, though dwellers in the roaring waste;
 And you, all shapes beside, that fishy be,—
 Some round, some flat, some long, all devilry,
Legless, unloving, infamously chaste:—

O scaly, slippery, wet, swift, staring wights,
 What is't ye do? What life lead? eh, dull goggles?

How do ye vary your vile days and nights?
   How pass your Sundays? Are ye still but joggles
In ceaseless wash? Still nought but gapes, and bites,
   And drinks, and stares, diversified with boggles?

A Fish Answers

Amazing monster! that, for aught I know,
   With the first sight of thee didst make our race
   For ever stare! O flat and shocking face,
Grimly divided from the breast below!
Thou that on dry land horribly dost go
   With a split body and most ridiculous pace,
   Prong after prong, disgracer of all grace,
Long-useless-finned, haired, upright, unwet, slow!

O breather of unbreathable, sword-sharp air,
   How canst exist? How bear thyself, thou dry
And dreary sloth? What particle canst share
   Of the only blessed life, the watery?
I sometimes see of ye an actual *pair*
   Go by! linked fin by fin! most odiously.

George Gordon, Lord Byron (1788–1824)

Sonnet on Chillon

*In his most elevated mood, Byron here exhibits the love of liberty,
the generosity and ardor of spirit, and the sense of individual man
at odds with repressive forces that made him seem for so long
an epitome of the romantic movement. Somewhat overblown in
effect, with its rhetorical emphasis, its exclamation marks, its
prison/altar metaphor, and its final invocation, the sonnet
nevertheless comes off successfully. Its language is simple and*

forceful, and the poet manages—though only just—to keep control of his tone and cadences and to fit them into the structure without dislocating it.

Eternal Spirit of the chainless Mind!
  Brightest in dungeons, Liberty! thou art,
  For there thy habitation is the heart—
The heart which love of thee alone can bind;
And when thy sons to fetters are consign'd—
  To fetters, and the damp vault's dayless gloom,
  Their country conquers with their martyrdom,
And Freedom's fame finds wings on every wind.
Chillon! thy prison is a holy place,
  And thy sad floor an altar; for 'twas trod,
Until his very steps have left a trace
  Worn, as if thy cold pavement were a sod,
By Bonnivard!—May none those marks efface!
  For they appeal from tyranny to God.

Percy Bysshe Shelley (1792–1822)

Ozymandias

This irregular but effective sonnet has been a thorn in the side of critics who insist on formal regularity of rhyme scheme. "Ozymandias," complains a twentieth-century American scholar, echoing nineteenth-century critics, "is destitute of symmetrical design." [2] *It is certainly true that Shelley's rhyme scheme— a b a b a c d c e f e g e g—is unique. It is also true that the dry tone, the single focus on the subject, and the powerful central irony expressed in lines 10–11 are singularly impressive and produce an effect quite different from that of Shelley's more characteristic*

[2] E. H. C. Oliphant, "Sonnet Structure: An Analysis," *Philological Quarterly*, XI, No. 1 (Jan. 1932), 138.

*lyrics. We are forced to conclude that conventional rules must
sometimes give way to the plenary inspiration of the poet.*

I met a traveller from an antique land
Who said: Two vast and trunkless legs of stone
Stand in the desert. Near them, on the sand,
Half sunk, a shattered visage lies, whose frown,
And wrinkled lip, and sneer of cold command,
Tell that its sculptor well those passions read
Which yet survive, stamped on these lifeless things,
The hand that mocked them and the heart that fed;
And on the pedestal these words appear:
"My name is Ozymandias, king of kings:
Look on my works, ye Mighty, and despair!"
Nothing beside remains. Round the decay
Of that colossal wreck, boundless and bare,
The lone and level sands stretch far away.

John Clare (1793–1864)

Signs of Winter

*Another instance of the wisdom of an empirical and not overly
pedantic approach to the sonnet. Written in unrhymed iambic
pentameter, by the "Northamptonshire Peasant Poet," this sonnet
presents a series of sharply observed scenes of rural life that give
the very look and atmosphere of late fall. Note the dialect words:*
knarls *is derived from a noun meaning a tangle or knot;*
swop, *at a blow, with sudden violence, is commonly used as an
adverb but here employed very effectively as verb;* mizzled *is again
an example of Clare's individual word usage. The noun or participle,
meaning "drizzle," is here used as adjective. The poem has a
homely, down-to-earth realism in its vocabulary and choice of detail
that makes an interesting contrast with Keats' ode "To Autumn."*

The cat runs races with her tail. The dog
Leaps o'er the orchard hedge and knarls the grass.
The swine run round and grunt and play with straw,
Snatching out hasty mouthfuls from the stack.
Sudden upon the elmtree tops the crow
Unceremonious visit pays and croaks,
Then swops away. From mossy barn the owl
Bobs hasty out—wheels round and, scared as soon,
As hastily retires. The ducks grow wild
And from a muddy pond fly up and wheel
A circle round the village and soon, tired,
Plunge in the pond again. The maids in haste
Snatch from the orchard hedge the mizzled clothes
And laughing hurry in to keep them dry.

John Keats (1795–1821)

On First Looking Into Chapman's Homer

*A beautiful example of Keats' early mastery of the sonnet. The
plain diction, simple, clear, and active syntax, and the central
analogy of the explorer and discoverer of new worlds concretely
convey Keats' delight, wonder, and exhilaration. The poem also
reveals two of the influences that made the early romantic movement
a second English Renaissance: the rediscovery of the ancient
classical world through its masterpieces of literature and art; and
the turning to the writers of the first Renaissance, the Elizabethan
and Jacobean poets and playwrights. These the writers of the
eighteenth century had neglected, tending for the most part to
consider them rude and barbarous.*

Much have I travell'd in the realms of gold,
　And many goodly states and kingdoms seen;
　Round many western islands have I been
Which bards in fealty to Apollo hold.

Oft of one wide expanse had I been told
   That deep-brow'd Homer ruled as his demesne:
   Yet did I never breathe its pure serene
Till I heard Chapman speak out loud and bold:
Then felt I like some watcher of the skies
   When a new planet swims into his ken;
Or like stout Cortez when with eagle eyes
   He stared at the Pacific—and all his men
Look'd at each other with a wild surmise—
   Silent, upon a peak in Darien.

On the Grasshopper and the Cricket

*A combination of realistic, observed nature with an ardent,
imaginative sense of the beauty and mystery of the natural world.
Note the balance and contrast in structure, scene, and image, as
firm in its own way as that of White's "To Night" (p. 78), yet far
less obtrusive. Opening with a general statement of the theme,
the octave describes the particular example of a summer scene. The
same statement of theme, now on a raised level of intensity, opens
the sestet, for the poetry of earth that, in the first line, "is never
dead," now becomes more active and lyrical with the participial
construction and feminine ending of "is ceasing never." The
repetition of theme is followed by another, parallel scene, this time
of a "lone winter evening," frosty, quiet, and solitary by contrast
with the noisy, hot, active summer day. The end leads the poet
himself, in imagination, back to the first scene, suggesting in
the very structure of the sonnet the cyclic alternation of the
seasons and the ebb and flow of natural rhythms.*

The poetry of earth is never dead:
   When all the birds are faint with the hot sun,
   And hide in cooling trees, a voice will run
From hedge to hedge about the new-mown mead;
That is the Grasshopper's—he takes the lead
   In summer luxury,—he has never done
   With his delights; for when tired out with fun,
He rests at ease beneath some pleasant weed.

The poetry of earth is ceasing never:
   On a lone winter evening, when the frost
      Has wrought a silence, from the stove there shrills
The Cricket's song, in warmth increasing ever,
   And seems to one, in drowsiness half lost,
      The Grasshopper's among some grassy hills.

On the Sea

*Compare this sonnet with Wordsworth's "The world is too much
with us . . ." (p. 75). Keats also sees nature as a source of
refreshment to eyes and ears vexed with the sights and sounds
of the modern world. But where Wordsworth concentrates on
man's relation to nature, Keats focuses on nature itself. The sestet,
with its somewhat oracular rhetoric and self-conscious exhortation,
is inferior to the octave's magical verbal re-creation of the
whispering, sucking tide rising and falling in rocky caverns and
the unearthly calm of the sea's moods of repose.*

It keeps eternal whisperings around
   Desolate shores, and with its mighty swell
   Gluts twice ten thousand caverns, till the spell
Of Hecate leaves them their old shadowy sound.
Often 't is in such gentle temper found,
   That scarcely will the very smallest shell
   Be mov'd for days from where it sometime fell,
When last the winds of Heaven were unbound.
O ye! who have your eyeballs vex'd and tir'd,
   Feast them upon the wideness of the Sea;
      O ye! whose ears are dinn'd with uproar rude,
   Or fed too much with cloying melody,—
      Sit ye near some old cavern's mouth, and brood
Until ye start, as if the sea-nymphs quired!

"When I have fears . . ."

*An example of the perfection Keats achieved in the English sonnet
form. Note how the fullness and abundance of harvest—the harvest*

of fame the young poet fears he may not live to reap—is rendered
in concrete terms in the first quatrain: glean'd, teeming, high pilèd,
rich garners, full-ripen'd grain. *In the second quatrain these concrete*
images change to a more abstract and symbolic picture: the starry
sky becomes a symbol of the "high romance" of poetry, the means
by which he hopes to achieve fame. In the sestet the poet faces the
equally poignant possibility of the loss of love, and the final lines
bring his reflections to that "nothingness" that is the polar opposite
of the rich fruition of beauty and passion he desires. This trancelike
contemplation by a young poet and lover of the passing away of
the things of this world is even more intolerably moving
than the end of "Bright star . . ."

When I have fears that I may cease to be
   Before my pen has glean'd my teeming brain,
Before high pilèd books, in charactry,
   Hold like rich garners the full-ripen'd grain;
When I behold, upon the night's starr'd face,
   Huge cloudy symbols of a high romance,
And think that I may never live to trace
   Their shadows, with the magic hand of chance;
And when I feel, fair creature of an hour!
   That I shall never look upon thee more,
Never have relish in the faery power
   Of unreflecting love;—then on the shore
Of the wide world I stand alone, and think
Till Love and Fame to nothingness do sink.

To Sleep

Interesting as an example of how Keats, at least once during his
annus mirabilis *of 1819, reverted to his earlier, less mature style.*
*Note the "soft" quality of the diction—*gloom-pleased, embower'd,
Enshaded, divine—*the repetitive invocation to sleep, the oddly*
particular enumeration of conscience as one of the cares from which
sleep must save him, and the painfully precious figure and diction
of the last two lines. The central image of sleep as an embalmer,
sealing "the hushed casket of my soul," is not one that would

commend itself to every taste. This is the Keats so much imitated
by poets of the later nineteenth and early twentieth century. The
rhyme scheme of this sonnet is very nearly as idiosyncratic as
that of "Ozymandias," but the two poems are otherwise
dissimilar in every respect.

O soft embalmer of the still midnight,
    Shutting, with careful fingers and benign,
Our gloom-pleased eyes, embower'd from the light,
    Enshaded in forgetfulness divine:
O soothest Sleep! if so it please thee, close,
    In midst of this thine hymn, my willing eyes,
Or wait the amen, ere thy poppy throws
    Around my bed its dewy charities;
    Then save me, or the passed day will shine
Upon my pillow, breeding many woes;
    Save me from curious conscience, that still lords
Its strength for darkness, burrowing like a mole;
    Turn the key deftly in the oiled wards,
And seal the hushed casket of my soul.

"Bright star . . ."

Supposed to have been written on shipboard as he sailed for
Italy and death, this poem is a flawless example of Keats' brief
perfection. The star, watching from the heavens the
undefilable purity of the sea and the new-fallen snow, is the eternal
and immutable counterpart of the human lover, "Pillow'd upon
my fair love's ripening breast"—a counterpart only in the poet's
imagination, for the human and heavenly levels are sharply
opposed. The human lover can only "would" he were as steadfast
as the star, "hung aloft the night" and forever watching with
unshut eyes. He would unite the steadfastness of the eternal
watcher and worshipper of earth with human love, subject to the
brief and passionate rhythms of blood and breath.
    The parallelism and antithesis of the star and lover is suggested
and reinforced by a variety of terms and images. The second line
emphasizes the star's position, its brightness, its aloofness from the

human level of the poet. Immediately, however, with the verb
watching *in the next line, the poet suggests the human level; the*
next phrase, "with eternal lids apart" carries out the suggestion of
a human watcher, yet simultaneously by the use of eternal *keeps*
the level of the star. The same effect is given in the next line:
"Nature's patient sleepless Eremite" suggests the human hermit or
worshipper, but the capitalization of Eremite *and the use of*
sleepless *remove it from a simply human connection. Both lines,*
besides suggesting the two levels, reinforce the steadfast *of the first*
line. The next four lines give us, curiously mingled, the heavenly
level, in the star's-eye view of the "moving waters," "earth's human
shores," and "mountains and moors"—present at once to its sight—
and the suggestion of purity in the "priestlike task," "pure
ablution," and the new-fallen snow, which is appropriate in
connection with the previous metaphor of the star as nature's eremite.

The No *of the ninth line marks an end to this thought sequence,*
echoing the Not *of the second line and reminding us that the*
lover wishes to emulate the steadfastness of the star on the human,
not the heavenly, level. Thus, though it employs the rhyme
scheme of the English sonnet, the poem exhibits the break at the
end of the octave and the turning to another aspect of the thought
characteristic of the Italian form. In the sestet, the lover's would-be
position is contrasted with that of the star in every particular save
that of "steadfastness." The lover, pillowed on the breast of his
beloved, "feels" its "soft fall and swell," while the star, "hung aloft
the night," "watches" the moving waters as they swell and ebb in
cosmic parallel with the girl's breath. The lover's relation to her is,
by direct implication, that of the star to nature; he is, on his human
level, her "patient sleepless Eremite," the worshipper of her beauty
and purity as the star on its heavenly level is the worshipper of
nature. The repetition of "for ever" in lines 11 and 12 emphasizes
the likeness—the desired likeness—of his steadfastness to that of the
star. "Awake for ever" at once suggests the "eternal lids apart" of
nature's Eremite, the star, while the "sweet unrest" of the lover
contrasts with the patience of the heavenly worshipper. "Still, still
to hear her tender-taken breath" gives the lover hearing *as before*
he felt—*close human contact in contrast with the eternal gazing from*
the heavens. And the final line is his acknowledgment that
steadfastness like the star's is not attainable in the transient world

*of time, change, and decay, but only in the eternal world after
death. The passion and the longing of the human spirit for a more
than human perfection have seldom been expressed so poignantly
and so richly, in a poem in which every word carries a full
load of meaning.*

Bright star, would I were steadfast as thou art!
   Not in lone splendour hung aloft the night,
And watching, with eternal lids apart,
   Like Nature's patient sleepless Eremite,
The moving waters at their priestlike task
   Of pure ablution round earth's human shores
Or gazing on the new soft fallen mask
   Of snow upon the mountains and the moors:
No—yet still steadfast, still unchangeable,
   Pillow'd upon my fair love's ripening breast,
To feel for ever its soft fall and swell,
   Awake for ever in a sweet unrest,
Still, still to hear her tender-taken breath,
And so live ever—or else swoon to death.

Thomas Lovell Beddoes (*1803–1849*)

To Tartar, a Terrier Beauty

*A charming and quite uncharacteristic poem by a minor romantic
remarkable for the exotic, not to say morbid and macabre, nature of
his more typical verse. The poem achieves its effect largely by the
humorous picture of the real dog at home in his doggy world,
similar to, yet different from, the human world, and by the contrast
of the subject itself with the elevated, artificial language and manner
in which it is treated. Note the odd rhyme scheme.*

Snow-drop of dogs, with ear of brownest dye,
Like the last orphan leaf of naked tree

Which shudders in bleak autumn; though by thee,
Of hearing careless and untutored eye,
Not understood articulate speech of men,
Nor marked the artificial mind of books—
The mortal's voice eternized by the pen—
Yet hast thou thought and language all unknown
To Babel's scholars; oft intensest looks,
Long scrutiny o'er some dark-veined stone
Dost thou bestow, learning dead mysteries
Of the world's birth-day; oft in eager tone
With quick-tailed fellows bandiest prompt replies,
Solicitudes canine, four-footed amities.

The Nineteenth Century

I

Wordsworth and Keats had restored the sonnet to an eminence and esteem it had not enjoyed since the time of Milton. Their example, however, was not immediately contagious. For a quarter of a century after the death of Keats, it seemed that no major poet took the form seriously or used it for more than brief and rather desultory ventures. The sonnet's structured conciseness did not suit Tennyson, who practiced the lyric of mood and melody so successfully. It did not suit Browning's more muscular rhythms and dramatic probing of character and situation. Arnold, who too soon abandoned verse for prose, produced a few sonnets but for the most part employed blank verse or the ten-line stanza of "Thyrsis" and "The Scholar-Gypsy" for narrative or meditative poems or experimented with a flexible unrhymed irregular verse. But if the three giants of mid-century neglected the sonnet, a poet as popular though not so great was to produce the first sonnet sequence on the theme of love that had been seen in England for more than two hundred years.

When Elizabeth Barrett Browning presented *Sonnets From The Portuguese* to her husband, she was by far the better-known poet of the two. This fact illuminates the tastes of the time, as the sonnets themselves reveal a good deal about the Victorian use of their romantic inheritance. The poems are conventional in form, diction, and imagery, sentimental in tone, and emotional to a degree embarrassing to a modern reader. Technically skillful as they are, these sonnets now seem overly personal and curiously abstract at the same time. Reading through them, it is easy to grow impatient with their sighs and their tears, their souls and their angels, their throbbing self-pity and wide-eyed raptures. The love Mrs. Browning celebrates, though connubial, is all purity and Platonic idealism. In some ways these sonnets recall Spenser's *Amoretti*; but in their emphasis on the personal they lack Spenser's dignity, and they have neither his lofty elevation of mood nor his glowing imagery. Nor do they, save now and then, have the intellectual or the spiritual toughness of the memorable Elizabethan sonnet. Matter and manner alike suited an age that was enthroning propriety as the goddess of the well-bred middle class, emphasizing domestic affections and virtues, and banishing both wit and passion to those twilight realms inhabited by the foreigner and the unregenerate.

The vogue of the sonnet sequence, which had so long been out of fashion, was henceforward to enjoy a modest revival, continuing well into the twentieth century. Most of the sequences, like Mrs. Browning's and the Elizabethan sequences, were on the theme of love. Outside of these, however, the nineteenth-century sonnet exhibited a variety of themes of which erotic love was only one. It suffered, as it had in all earlier periods, from indiscriminate use by inferior poets until at the end of the century Edwin Arlington Robinson was calling:

> Oh for a poet—for a beacon bright
>
> . . . . .
>
> To put these little sonnet-men to flight
> Who fashion, in a shrewd mechanic way,
> Songs without souls, that flicker for a day,
> To vanish in irrevocable night.

But it did not suffer, like the Elizabethan sonnet, from too much concentration on one convention and one topic. In form, in diction, in imagery it lived, like most Victorian poetry, on the inherited capital of the past. The contribution of the nineteenth century was to demonstrate the versatility of the form, its easy adaptation to a whole gamut of moods, and a variety of temperaments and topics. The sonnets of this century are a mirror in which the central attitudes, problems, and preoccupations of a troubled age are reflected in microcosm.

II

The characteristic note of the Victorian sonnet is melancholy. Pride, passion, indignation, exaltation—the hallmarks of fine sonnets in earlier times—give way to uncertainty, insecurity, anxiety, sadness. Few indeed record moods of affirmation or proclaim a positive response to the challenges of life. They are pervaded by a sense of loneliness, isolation, and alienation. Love is no longer joy or agony, but a refuge from the pains and perplexities of life and the uncertainties of the cosmos. Tradition and the past are invoked as a counterbalance to the lesser world of the present. Faith itself is no longer a living reality to be sought as a source of strength. Wistfully the Victorians cling to or angrily they discard old modes of thought and feeling now under assault by the social and intellectual forces of the age.

Thomas Hood's "Silence" and "Death" are typical of many Victorian sonnets in their choice of abstract philosophical subjects, their reflective and melancholy tone, their focus on what is essentially a subjective mood of self-indulgent sadness. They exhibit the narrowing of content and the lessening of energy of the romantic movement that is characteristic of all nineteenth-century poetry. Nature as a revelation of spiritual truth, nature however beautiful, is increasingly seen as disjoined from, and indifferent to, man; and increasingly the emphasis is on man's plight in an alien universe: "I, a stranger and afraid,/In a world I never made." So A. E. Housman, a minor but distinguished late Victorian, expressed the feeling that begins early in the century and runs strongly throughout.

The main reasons for this malaise can be easily perceived by today's reader; for though its ramifications are many and complex, it is no less obvious now. The Victorian period was the beginning of the modern world. Industrialization was altering the face of the land, changing age-old social and personal patterns and relationships. Science and scholarship together were mounting a frontal assault on the ancient authority of Scripture and the church. The revolution that had begun with Copernicus could no longer be evaded or denied, and its implications were shaking the foundations of faith. All around them the embattled Victorians saw the old bulwarks crumbling: faith in God and His cosmos, faith in man and his society. And the poets of the age, major and minor alike, reflected according to their varying temperaments the climate of doubt, anxiety, and distress.

Old beliefs and old pieties continued to exercise their authority on some poets, as on most less articulate humans, but their expression had a different ring from the faith of the past. When we compare Trench's "Returning Home" or Tennyson-Turner's "The Lattice At Sunrise" or Marston's "Immortality" with Donne or Herbert, we are aware not only of a difference in talent, but even more of a difference in the poet's conception of and relation to his subject. Religion was indeed *personal* to Donne, terrifyingly personal, involving the eternal welfare of his soul. But it was a personal relationship to a great reality existing quite objectively, apart from him and his relationship to it. For the Victorian poets, religion had become not a matter of faith nor salvation but of *mood*. It was intellectually vaguer, with none of Donne's vigor and precision of thought and image, and it was softer and more sentimental in feeling, a legacy from the evangelical current of the eighteenth century. The imperative energy of evangelism seems to have been diluted, however, like the intellectual energy of dogma and creed. As there was no longer any real theology to give structure and image, so there was no real struggle, no agony, no inexorable command laid on the soul. Christianity was losing its hold on the mind and the will and continued to speak only to the heart.

Some poets, of whom Longfellow is the best example, sought in the culture of the past the beauty, peace, and solace denied them by their own world. His are polished verses in which the voice of a tradition speaks both in form and content. Technically they are flawless, executed with the competence of a master craftsman. The literature, the art, the religion of the past is invoked as what Robert Frost was later to call "a momentary stay against confusion." Chaucer, Dante, the architecture and the rituals of the Catholic Church were to Longfellow sources of aesthetic pleasure, reassurance, and a sense of continuity and permanence amid change. There is in these sonnets no strong emotion, no sense of conflict, no statement of faith or unfaith. They are calm and gentle, responsive to beauty both sensuous and spiritual, elevated in mood but never impassioned. There are no fireworks here either of heart or mind, no hidden effects, no surprises or shocks. Everything they contain is apparent on a first reading. They are the essence of what Hopkins was to call "Parnassian" poetry, verses in which a gifted poet thoroughly conversant with a tradition speaks out of his skill and his learning, not under the spur of a primary and individual creative impulse.

Poe's sonnet "To Science" states much more explicitly the nature of the threat perceived by sensitive minds in the rapid changes from the world of the past to that of the present. It became ever more widely feared and more deeply felt that science and industry between them were creating a society in which men could not live with themselves, with their fellows, with nature, or with God. This fear accounts in large part for the growing alienation of the artist from society, an alienation already implicit in some of Tennyson's early verse, more apparent in Rossetti's, almost an article of faith with the poets of the nineties, and evident well into the twentieth century.

III

With Dante Gabriel Rossetti and his sister Christina, the Victorian sonnet came fully into its own. Always excepting Hopkins, the Rossettis are the greatest sonneteers of the later century. Dante Gabriel's *The House of Life* is the most distinguished sequence on the theme of love since *Astrophel and Stella*. It is, however, as different from Sidney's verse as two very different periods and even more different temperaments could make it.

In *The House of Life* Rossetti, exploring his own emotional experience, embodies a whole philosophy of life and of love. It is not love for a single woman that he celebrates but love itself as he imagined and knew it. In these sonnets he reveals his conception of ideal beauty as embodied in womanhood, his natural Platonism, his temperament in which sensuality is mingled with a vague but ardent mysticism, and a longing for spiritual fulfillment through sexual love. The sequence is part of a larger work that Rossetti planned but never completed. As it stands, it is a series of sonnets divided into two parts, "Youth and Change," and "Change and Fate," with no very distinct principle of grouping. Love, lord of the House of Life (*House* used here in a vaguely astrological sense), is presented in many forms—physical and spiritual. The sonnets move from passion and adoration to love won but frustrate, to premonitions of separation, loss, and death, to brooding over unfulfilled hopes, self-doubt and self-reproach, to longing for death and questionings of a future life, concluding with "the one hope."

Rossetti's sonnets reveal much about the direction Victorian poetry was taking and the changes in the romantic inheritance as it moved from the early to the late nineteenth century. He stands somewhere between Keats, who very much influenced him, and the poets of the 1890s. Like Keats he worships beauty, but unlike the earlier poet's wider vision, he sees beauty embodied not in the world and in the eternal forms of art, but in woman. Unlike the three central Victorian poets, Rossetti has released his verse from all ethical or social preoccupations; and unlike the poets who followed him, he has no need to rebel against the modern world or against religious belief. The latter he uses for its emotional and decorative values, entirely excluding the question of faith or creed. The former he shuts out of his work completely. Great as was his talent and his achievement in his successful poems, Rossetti reveals the narrowing of perspective, theme, content, and attitude that marks Victorian romanticism as it develops through the century.

Christina Rossetti combined a poetic talent almost equal to her brother's and a poetic integrity greater than his—a claim she would never have made—with an outlook and a nature far narrower, less complex, more consistent. Possessed and dominated by Christian faith more than any other poet of the time, she is the lyricist of the conflict between the world and the soul. She dismisses the joy and sensuous delights of life that she desires but fears as a brief prelude to everlasting sin. Her verse is all in a minor key, exquisitely wrought but sad, world-weary, preoccupied with loss and death. All is subordinate to a central mood, a few themes.

Christina Rossetti's interest in the sonnet form, like her brother's, was inevitable. Their family was deeply read in Italian literature and used the sonnet as a literary exercise. Like Dante Gabriel, Christina keeps to the Petrarchan form and explains the theme of her sequence *Monna Innominata* in Petrarchan terms: a lady of the Provençal Renaissance period is loved by a poet as Beatrice and Laura were later loved, but a barrier not explicitly described separates the lady and her lover and shadows and frustrates their love. Despite this pretence of a dramatic setting, the sonnets are in no sense either a drama or a narrative, but like most of her verse a revelation of Christina's own moods. Whether, as some of her brother's undoubtedly do, they record real experience is a matter of dispute. Nor is the question of any real importance for a reader of her poetry. Whatever may be discovered or inferred about Christina's life—and almost as many efforts to discover a real basis for her poetry of love and renunciation have been made as in the somewhat similar case of Emily Dickinson—the merits of her verse are as palpable as its limitations. Her sonnets are pellucid in diction, simple and clear in syntax and structure. Their cadences and rhythms are managed with masterly control and economy. They are restrained by clarity and simplicity from the sentimentality and over-emotion-alism that mar Mrs. Browning's verse. Like her lyrics in general, Christina's sonnets are the "musical but melancholy chime" that sings one song and that one perfectly.

IV

While the minor poets of the later nineteenth century were ex-pressing the anxieties of the age in sonnets that were—however skillful—conventional in form, diction, and image and often all but indistinguishable in manner, a greater writer was shaping the sonnet to his own highly individual utterance. The poems of Thomas Hardy present a remarkable contrast to those of the Rossettis or for that matter any other of the Victorian poets. Hardy's long life did not end until 1928, but all his poetry—early or late—is unmis-takably Victorian both in form and content. Yet he struck so in-dividual a note that it is not possible to mistake his voice for that of anyone else. This is partly because the diction and syntax he uses are peculiarly his own. But it is not merely a matter of dialect words or of his highly idiosyncratic use of a stock vocabulary or of odd constructions, though his style is marked by all of these. It is a matter of tone, of attitude, of feeling that stamp as Hardy's own even verses on conventional or commonplace subjects.

Hardy was sensitive to the point of agony; but it is the pain of mankind he laments, not his own. His poems are full of pity for men at odds with the universe, with each other, with themselves. Hardy's tender heart was yoked in harness with a cool, clear, some-what sardonic mind that persisted in looking unflinchingly at what seemed to him to be the truth. And what he saw, equally with the pain, was the tragicomedy of the gulf between men's views, hopes, and desires and the inexorable realities of the cosmos. The dynamic tension between pity and irony, neither diluted by the presence of the other, both operating under full pressure and simultaneously, is what gives Hardy's verse its distinctive flavor.

"The village atheist brooding and blaspheming over the village idiot" is G. K. Chesterton's description of him. But this is neither fair nor true. Like most of the sensitive minds of his century, Hardy was agonized by the conflict between old values and new percep-tions. His heart still desired the God of his fathers, still yearned for the beauty of holiness and the solace of divine love; but what he saw and what he had learned forced him to reject faith and hope, though never charity. It was a dilemma all the Victorians felt, though none faced it quite as Hardy did. His way was to grasp firmly both horns of the dilemma. He abandoned neither pity and love nor his vision of the haphazard cruelties of the world. The absolute integrity of his verse is its most striking feature, and one is compelled finally to describe it not in aesthetic but in moral and intellectual terms. At its best, it is very good indeed. But our first and final response to Hardy is not admiration for the skill of an artist but love for the honesty, the courage, and the tenderness of a man.

V

The most original sonneteer of the nineteenth century—perhaps the most original in the long history of the sonnet—was not known to the great majority of poets and readers until the third decade of the twentieth century. By an accident of long-delayed publication, Gerard Manley Hopkins became in effect not a Victorian but a modern poet whose work has markedly influenced other modern poets. Criticism has, even now, not entirely caught up with him; and his position in the history of English poetry is still to be fully assessed. In 1941 the first edition of *The Concise Cambridge History of English Literature,* while acknowledging Hopkins' "incandescent intensity of apprehension," dismissed him in these terms: "nothing of him remains but intimations of what he might have become." In 1971 the second edition of the same volume described Hopkins as "the man whom some modern critics, including the present writer, hold to be unquestionably the greatest poet of the Victorian age." Between the two verdicts—neither of which, incidentally, is likely to be the final word—lies a revolution in poetic taste and sensibility. It was a revolution that began in the years immediately after the end of World War I and continues to our own day. Its history belongs to the literary history of the twentieth century. But the poet whose experiments, unique in their time, very much influenced that revolution, died in 1889, thirty years before his verse was known to anyone save a handful of close friends.

Born in 1844, Gerard Manley Hopkins was converted to Catholicism while a student at Oxford, under the influence of John Henry, later Cardinal, Newman. Hopkins entered the Jesuit order and spent the rest of his short life as a priest, teaching and working in the service of the Church. Poetry was thus his avocation, not his vocation. Indeed, he had abandoned writing on entering the priesthood and resumed it again only at the suggestion of his superiors. His work existed in manuscript and his theories of prosody mostly in letters to his close friend Robert Bridges. At his death, his poetry was entrusted to Bridges, who published a few poems in anthologies, but waited until 1918, when he judged the time was finally ripe, before publishing Hopkins' major work in volume form. Not until the thirties was Hopkins' originality perceived by twentieth-century poets. And, as the example of the *Cambridge History* shows, critical appreciation waited still longer. A fully informed and balanced judgment of Hopkins' achievement is still in process.

Hopkins' peculiar poetic genius ran counter to the whole nineteenth-century romantic tradition. He combined great technical originality with remarkable observation of nature, intensity of feeling, and a mind informed by Catholic doctrine and inspired by passionate faith. Poets and critics who do not share his faith have tended to appreciate him more for form than content, more for his technical brilliance than for the use to which he put it. But Hopkins' techniques, however striking, cannot finally be separated from his religious subjects and purposes. It is thought and feeling that give his poetry its structure and effect, and his style is integral and subordinate to intellectual and emotional content.

The hallmark of Hopkins' style is his use of what he called "sprung rhythm." Simply described, this refers to a metrical foot in which one stressed syllable may be combined with a varying number of unstressed syllables. Hopkins' greatest skill is exhibited in managing the irregular spacing of stresses thus permitted in lines ranging from only four heavily accented syllables accompanied by no light ones, to as many as sixteen syllables of which, again, only four are stressed. These varying feet and lines are united by the poet into rhythmical patterns wholly different in effect from those produced by traditional metrical forms.

Hopkins' originality can be seen at its best in his variations on the conventional sonnet form. It will be apparent that his use of sprung rhythm violates the strict rules for good sonnets set forth by nineteenth-century critics like William Sharp and Hall Caine and, later, by T. W. H. Crosland. These legislators insisted, above all, on the iambic decasyllabic line and drew up careful guidelines for the management of pauses within octave and sestet. Hopkins' management of the pauses and stresses of his irregular feet and lines creates a nervous, abrupt, exclamatory, dramatic texture and a rhythmic pattern greatly at variance with the traditional sonnet. That his innovations proceeded from full knowledge of tradition and much hard thought is attested to by his correspondence with Bridges. Hopkins was not an untaught and wayward talent but something much rarer: an original creative mind fully aware of what he was attempting to do in his verse.

In addition to his basic metrical experiments, Hopkins' poetry is marked by a fresh, highly individual vocabulary very different from the language of nineteenth-century romantic poetry. He draws heavily on Anglo-Saxon word stock and is particularly fond of "kennings"—compound descriptive terms, such as *bone-house* for body —of obsolete native words, or archaisms, provincialisms, and coinages. Like the Anglo-Saxon poets, he uses alliteration and assonance to bind together rhythmic and syntactical units; and he harmonizes and counterpoints his verse with related groups of consonant clusters. He persistently violates normal syntax and dispenses with ordinary links and transitions, employing constructions that are abrupt, elliptical, and frequently difficult to follow at first sight. By all these means Hopkins charges his verse with intense energy; energy of word, of movement, of thought, of soul. His techniques make vivid to eye, ear, and mind his intense response to what he called the "inscapes" of nature—its distinctive designs and patterns. They brilliantly dramatize Christian doctrine, and they create by their very rhythms the poet's tortured wrestling with his own spiritual distress. Despite his occasional vice of "queerness," to use his own word, his best verse has irresistible force and power—physical, psychic, and poetic.

It is easy for even the casual reader to perceive the electric energy, the unusual rhythms, the odd words, and word usage of Hopkins' sonnets. It is not, perhaps, so easy to perceive how boldly and precisely the poet uses rhythm, word, symbol, and image to dramatize abstract thought. The sonnet "God's Grandeur," for example, is more than a celebration of the God whose Creation, unlike man's, is perpetually renewed. Its dramatic structure is given by specific Christian doctrines—the Trinity, Original Sin, the Incarnation, the Crucifixion, the Resurrection—suggested in word and image.

In much the same way, other sonnets dramatize aspects of Christian thought and feeling. "The Caged Skylark" turns on one of the most mysterious of Christian doctrines. The contrast between the bird caged and the bird at home in its own nest symbolizes the difference between man imprisoned in mortal flesh and man as he will be after the resurrection of the body. Hopkins' famous "The Windhover" dramatizes the difference between action and passion, between the kingdom of this world and the kingdom of the spirit, by the contrast between the falcon, "kingdom of daylight's dauphin," and Christ, chevalier of the spiritual world. Careful reading of sonnets like these will show how futile it is to attempt to separate Hopkins' technical devices from the whole thrust of his poetic purpose.

VI

When Hopkins died in 1889, his poetry unknown, the romantic current that had flowed through English poetry for more than a century found itself temporarily in a backwater. The poetry of the twentieth century was to prove romanticism far from exhausted; but for the moment it was at a standstill, its original energy lost, its vision limited and distorted. In the poets of the nineties—Wilde, Dowson, Johnson, Douglas—can be seen the culmination of tendencies long apparent in the earlier part of the century as well as fresh influences from the French symbolist poets. Tennyson's early "Palace of Art," Rossetti's mystical and sensuous *House of Life,* Swinburne's feverish rejection of conventional values and attitudes, Pater's famous definition of the successful life—"to burn always with this hard, gem-like flame, to maintain this ecstasy"—the French doctrine of *l'art pour l'art:* all these had become the gospel of sensation at any price, an amoral aestheticism.

It is not as surprising as it might seem that these poets reveal in their verse and in their lives as well a strong pull toward Catholicism. Their religious impulse, however, was very different from Hopkins' faith. The nineties poets were attracted by the beauty and the mysticism of Catholic ritual, and they found in Catholicism and in the medieval world with which they associated it a bulwark against the ugly Philistinism of their own world. Similar tendencies had displayed themselves in poetry throughout the century. What is new is the passion and defiance with which these poets challenged the modern industrial and mercantile world as Victoria's long reign drew to an end. They emphasized moments of passion and sensation for their own sake and excluded larger impersonal concerns; they introduced themes hitherto excluded from verse; they were interested in strange and abnormal states of mind; and they constantly gave utterance to a sense of world-weariness and of sin. The few sonnets included here are miniatures of the world of the 1890s and of a movement that extended far outside poetry. The essence of it is perhaps best conveyed not by the poetry of the time but by Aubrey Beardsley's drawings in the *Yellow Book* and the *Savoy* and in his illustrations to Wilde's *Salome,* in Beardsley's *sub rosa* novel *Under the Hill,* and in such symbolic public events as Wilde's trial in 1895.

Thomas Hood (1799–1846)

Silence

Note the form—Wyatt's Italian sonnet with a well-defined break between octave and sestet but closing with a couplet. Though there was no fundamental change or experiment with the sonnet form until Hopkins, the nineteenth-century poets used the traditional patterns freely, with many variations in the handling of rhyme scheme and the relation of the parts of the sonnet. The critics and anthologists of the period complain bitterly of this freedom and often harshly criticize departures from what they regard as the established orthodoxy of the Italian sonnet. In this sonnet, the long alexandrine of the last line is such a departure and materially strengthens the poem. The juxtaposed heavy stresses in each half of the final line are particularly effective in fitting cadence to mood and subject.

There is a silence where hath been no sound;
   There is a silence where no sound may be
   In the cold grave—under the deep, deep sea,
Or in wide desert where no life is found,
Which hath been mute, and still must sleep profound:
   No voice is hushed—not life treads silently,
   But clouds and cloudy shadows wander free
That never spoke, over the idle ground.
But in green ruins, in the desolate walls
   Of antique palaces, where Man hath been,
Though the dun fox, or wild hyæna, calls,
   And owls, that flit continually between,
Shriek to the echo, and the low winds moan.
There the true Silence is, self-conscious and alone.

Death

*A rare revival of the Spenserian sonnet rhyme scheme, used
very infrequently since Spenser's day.*

It is not death, that sometime in a sigh
   This eloquent breath shall take its speechless flight;
That sometime these bright stars, that now reply
   In sunlight to the sun, shall set in night,
   That this warm conscious flesh shall perish quite,
And all life's ruddy springs forget to flow;
   That thoughts shall cease, and the immortal sprite
Be lapped in alien clay and laid below;
It is not death to know this,—but to know
   That pious thoughts, which visit at new graves
In tender pilgrimage, will cease to go
   So duly and so oft,—and when grass waves
Over the past-away, there may be then
No resurrection in the minds of men.

Elizabeth Barrett Browning (1806–1861)

FROM *Sonnets From the Portuguese*

1–"I thought once how Theocritus . . ."

An instance of Mrs. Browning's tendency to celebrate the experience of love in curiously abstract terms. The reference is to the fifteenth idyll of Theocritus, Greek writer of pastoral poetry.

I thought once how Theocritus had sung
Of the sweet years, the dear and wished-for years,
Who each one in a gracious hand appears
To bear a gift for mortals, old or young:
And, as I mused it in his antique tongue,
I saw, in gradual vision through my tears,
The sweet, sad years, the melancholy years,
Those of my own life, who by turns had flung
A shadow across me. Straightway I was 'ware,
So weeping, how a mystic Shape did move
Behind me, and drew me backward by the hair,
And a voice said in mastery, while I strove,—
'Guess now who holds thee?'—'Death,' I said. But, there,
The silver answer rang, . . 'Not Death, but Love.'

6–"Go from me . . ."

Go from me. Yet I feel that I shall stand
Henceforward in thy shadow. Nevermore
Alone upon the threshold of my door
Of individual life, I shall command
The uses of my soul, nor lift my hand
Serenely in the sunshine as before,
Without the sense of that which I forbore, . .

Thy touch upon the palm. The widest land
Doom takes to part us, leaves thy heart in mine
With pulses that beat double. What I do
And what I dream include thee, as the wine
Must taste of its own grapes. And when I sue
God for myself, He hears that name of thine,
And sees within my eyes the tears of two.

20–"Beloved, my Beloved . . ."

*The rather strained analogy here is characteristic of the poet's
striving for overemphatic emotional statement.*

Beloved, my Beloved, when I think
That thou wast in the world a year ago,
What time I sat alone here in the snow
And saw no footprint, heard the silence sink
No moment at thy voice, . . . but, link by link,
Went counting all my chains as if that so
They never could fall off at any blow
Struck by thy possible hand . . . why, thus I drink
Of life's great cup of wonder! Wonderful,
Never to feel thee thrill the day or night
With personal act or speech,—nor ever cull
Some prescience of thee with the blossoms white
Thou sawest growing! Atheists are as dull,
Who cannot guess God's presence out of sight.

22–"When our two souls . . ."

*Despite the "soft" diction, the management of the pauses within
the line gives a more athletic movement and the conclusion a more
tough-minded effect than is usual with Mrs. Browning.*

When our two souls stand up erect and strong,
Face to face, silent, drawing nigh and nigher,
Until the lengthening wings break into fire

At either curvèd point,—what bitter wrong
Can the earth do to us, that we should not long
Be here contented? Think. In mounting higher,
The angels would press on us and aspire
To drop some golden orb of perfect song
Into our deep, dear silence. Let us stay
Rather on earth, Belovèd,—where the unfit
Contrarious moods of men recoil away
And isolate pure spirits, and permit
A place to stand and love in for a day,
With darkness and the death-hour rounding it.

43–"How do I love thee . . ."

*Much admired in its day, but its abstract metaphors and
heavy, earnest emotion unqualified by simplicity, irony, or wit
now date badly.*

How do I love thee? Let me count the ways.
I love thee to the depth and breadth and height
My soul can reach, when feeling out of sight
For the ends of Being and ideal Grace.
I love thee to the level of every day's
Most quiet need, by sun and candlelight.
I love thee freely, as men strive for Right;
I love thee purely, as they turn from Praise.
I love thee with the passion put to use
In my old griefs, and with my childhood's faith.
I love thee with a love I seemed to lose
With my lost saints,—I love thee with the breath,
Smiles, tears, of all my life!—and, if God choose,
I shall but love thee better after death.

Richard Chevenix Trench (*1807–1886*)

Gibraltar

Another instance of the cavalier indifference of many poets of the period to strict rules. Note here the irregular rhyme scheme and the break into equal seven-line parts rather than octave and sestet. Twentieth-century readers may well wonder whether anyone will ever again be able to feel the emotions Trench here describes.

England, we love thee better than we know—
And this I learned, when after wanderings long
'Mid people of another stock and tongue,
I heard again thy martial music blow,
And saw thy gallant children to and fro
Pace, keeping ward at one of those huge gates,
Twin giants watching the Herculean Straits.
When first I came in sight of that brave show,
It made my very heart within me dance,
To think that thou thy proud foot shouldst advance
Forward so far into the mighty sea;
Joy was it and exultation to behold
Thine ancient standard's rich emblazonry,
A glorious picture by the wind unrolled.

Returning Home

To leave unseen so many a glorious sight,
To leave so many lands unvisited,
To leave so many worthiest books unread,
Unrealized so many visions bright;—
Oh! wretched yet inevitable spite
Of our brief span, that we must yield our breath,

And wrap us in the unfeeling coil of death,
So much remaining of unproved delight.
But hush, my soul, and vain regrets, be stilled;
Find rest in Him who is the complement
Of whatsoe'er transcends our mortal doom,
Of baffled hope and unfulfilled intent;
In the clear vision and aspèct of whom
All longings and all hopes shall be fulfilled.

Charles Tennyson-Turner (1808–1879)

The Steam-Threshing Machine

*Tennyson-Turner, a clergyman, was the older brother of the more
famous Alfred, later Lord Tennyson and Poet Laureate, and
co-author with him of a first volume entitled* Poems By Two
Brothers. *"The Steam-Threshing Machine" is a valiant effort to
assimilate the present world of industry and science to the revered
past. The allusion is to Virgil, greatest poet of Roman times, whose*
Bucolics *and* Georgics *idealize aspects of rural life.*

Flush with the pond the lurid furnace burn'd
At eve, while smoke and vapour fill'd the yard;
The gloomy winter sky was dimly starr'd,
The fly-wheel with a mellow murmur turn'd;
While, ever rising on its mystic stair
In the dim light, from secret chambers borne,
The straw of harvest, sever'd from the corn,
Climb'd, and fell over, in the murky air.
I thought of mind and matter, will and law,
And then of him, who set his stately seal
Of Roman words on all the forms he saw
Of old-world husbandry: *I* could but feel
With what a rich precision *he* would draw
The endless ladder, and the booming wheel!

The Lattice at Sunrise

As on my bed at dawn I mused and prayed,
    I saw my lattice prankt upon the wall,
    The flaunting leaves and flitting birds withal—
A sunny phantom interlaced with shade;
"Thanks be to heaven!" in happy mood I said,
    "What sweeter aid my matins could befall
Than this fair glory from the East hath made?
    What holy sleights hath God, the Lord of all,
To bid us feel and see! we are not free
    To say we see not, for the glory comes
Nightly and daily, like the flowing sea;
    His lustre pierceth through the midnight glooms;
And, at prime hour, behold! He follows me
    With golden shadows to my secret rooms!"

Henry Wadsworth Longfellow (1807–1882)

Nature

As a fond mother, when the day is o'er,
    Leads by the hand her little child to bed,
    Half willing, half reluctant to be led
And leave his broken playthings on the floor,
Still gazing at them through the open door,
    Not wholly reassured and comforted
    By promises of others in their stead,
Which, though more splendid, may not please him more;
So Nature deals with us, and takes away
    Our playthings one by one, and by the hand
    Leads us to rest so gently that we go
Scarce knowing if we wish to go or stay,

Being too full of sleep to understand
  How the unknown transcends the what we know.

Chaucer

An old man in a lodge within a park;
  The chamber walls depicted all around
  With portraitures of huntsman, hawk, and hound.
  And the hurt deer. He listeneth to the lark,
Whose song comes with the sunshine through the dark
  Of painted glass in leaden lattice bound;
  He listeneth and he laugheth at the sound,
  Then writeth in a book like any clerk.
He is the poet of the dawn, who wrote
  The Canterbury Tales, and his old age
  Made beautiful with song; and as I read
I hear the crowing cock, I hear the note
  Of lark and linnet, and from every page
  Rise odours of plough'd field or flowery mead.

FROM *Divina Commedia*

1–"Oft have I seen at some cathedral door"

Oft have I seen at some cathedral door
A laborer, pausing in the dust and heat,
Lay down his burden, and with reverent feet
Enter, and cross himself, and on the floor
Kneel to repeat his paternoster o'er;
Far off the noises of the world retreat;
The loud vociferations of the street
Become an undistinguishable roar.
So, as I enter here from day to day,
And leave my burden at this minster gate,
Kneeling in prayer, and not ashamed to pray,
The tumult of the time disconsolate
To inarticulate murmurs dies away,
While the eternal ages watch and wait.

5–"I lift mine eyes . . ."

I lift mine eyes, and all the windows blaze
With forms of Saints and holy men who died,
Here martyred and hereafter glorified;
And the great Rose upon its leaves displays
Christ's Triumph, and the angelic roundelays,
With splendor upon splendor multiplied;
And Beatrice again at Dante's side
No more rebukes, but smiles her words of praise.
And then the organ sounds, and unseen choirs
Sing the old Latin hymns of peace and love
And benedictions of the Holy Ghost;
And the melodious bells among the spires
O'er all the house-tops and through heaven above
Proclaim the elevation of the Host!

Edgar Allan Poe (1809–1849)

To Science

Compare this sonnet with Wordsworth's "The world is too much with us . . ." (p. 75). Here it is science, rather than industrialization and commerce, that has deprived the poet of his ancient realm, the world of the imagination.

Science! true daughter of Old Time thou art!
  Who alterest all things with thy peering eyes.
Why preyest thou thus upon the poet's heart,
  Vulture, whose wings are dull realities?
How should he love thee? or how deem thee wise,
  Who wouldst not leave him in his wandering
To seek for treasure in the jewelled skies,

Albeit he soared with an undaunted wing?
Hast thou not dragged Diana from her car?
  And driven the Hamadryad from the wood
To seek a shelter in some happier star?
  Hast thou not torn the Naiad from her flood,
The Elfin from the green grass, and from me
  The summer dream beneath the tamarind tree?

Westland Marston (1819–1890)

Immortality
An Inference

If I had lived ere seer or priest unveiled
  A life to come, methinks that, knowing thee,
  I should have guessed thine immortality;
For Nature, giving instincts, never failed
To give the ends they point to. Never quailed
  The swallow, through air-wilds, o'er tracts of sea,
  To chase the summer; seeds that prisoned be
Dream of and find the daylight. Unassailed
  By doubt, impelled by yearnings for the main,
The creature river-born doth there emerge;
  So thou, with thoughts and longings which our earth
Can never compass in its narrow verge,
  Shalt the fit region of thy spirit gain,
And death fulfil the promptings of thy birth.

Matthew Arnold (1822–1888)

To Shakespeare

A fine specimen of the sonnet as eulogy. This poem and Wordsworth's sonnet to Milton make an interesting contrast with a twentieth-century example such as Cumming's tribute to Chaucer (p. 200).

Others abide our question. Thou art free.
We ask and ask—Thou smilest and art still,
Out-topping knowledge. For the loftiest hill,
Who to the stars uncrowns his majesty,

Planting his stedfast footsteps in the sea,
Making the heaven of heavens his dwelling-place,
Spares but the cloudy border of his base
To the foil'd searching of mortality;

And thou, who didst the stars and sunbeams know,
Self-school'd, self-scann'd, self-honour'd, self-secure,
Didst walk on earth unguess'd at.—Better so!

All pains the immortal spirit must endure,
All weakness which impairs, all griefs which bow,
Find their sole voice in that victorious brow.

George Meredith (1828–1909)

Lucifer in Starlight

Note the fine "Miltonic" quality, the cosmic scope and elevation of tone, and the magnificent last line with its sense of the grandeur of nature's laws.

On a starred night Prince Lucifer uprose.
  Tired of his dark dominion swung the fiend
  Above the rolling ball in cloud part screened,
Where sinners hugged their spectre of repose.
Poor prey to his hot fit of pride were those.
  And now upon his western wing he leaned,
  Now his huge bulk o'er Africa careened,
Now the black planet shadowed Arctic snows.
Soaring through wider zones that pricked his scars
  With memory of the old revolt from Awe,
He reached a middle height, and at the stars,
  Which are the brain of heaven, he looked, and sank
  Around the ancient track marched, rank on rank,
The army of unalterable law.

FROM *Modern Love*

Both poems are from a sequence of fifty sixteen-line stanzas that have a definite sonnet-like effect. They are very different from Rossetti's The House of Life, *or for that matter, from any other sonnet sequence written in English. The whole is the story of a disastrous marriage, each separate poem dwelling on a single mood or incident in the narrative. Meredith avoids both the mystical and the moral, striking instead—as the title suggests—a peculiarly modern note. He combines psychological analysis of the lovers'*

*varying moods and experiences—intimate, realistic, and very personal
in tone—with natural images so used as to become symbols that
comment in a grand and impersonal manner on love and life.*

47–"We saw the swallows . . ."

*A perfect blend of mood and setting. This poem furnishes an
interesting contrast with Wordsworth's "Composed Upon
Westminster Bridge" (p. 70). Note how differently each poet uses
scene to express a moment of vision.*

We saw the swallows gathering in the sky,
And in the osier-isle we heard them noise.
We had not to look back on summer joys,
Or forward to a summer of bright dye:
But in the largeness of the evening earth
Our spirits grew as we went side by side.
The hour became her husband and my bride.
Love that had robbed us so, thus blessed our dearth!
The pilgrims of the year waxed very loud
In multitudinous chatterings, as the flood
Full brown came from the West, and like pale blood
Expanded to the upper crimson cloud.
Love that had robbed us of immortal things,
This little moment mercifully gave,
Where I have seen across the twilight wave
The swan sail with her young beneath her wings.

50–"Thus piteously Love closed what he begat"

*Here Meredith combines, as he often does in this sequence,
psychological analysis with more general philosophic comment.
Note how the end of the stanza presents us with an image of man's
ignorant, helpless, and lonely existence in the midst of a menacing
universe.*

Thus piteously Love closed what he begat:
The union of this ever-diverse pair!

These two were rapid falcons in a snare,
Condemned to do the flitting of the bat.
Lovers beneath the singing sky of May,
They wandered once; clear as the dew on flowers:
But they fed not on the advancing hours:
Their hearts held cravings for the buried day.
Then each applied to each that fatal knife,
Deep questioning, which probes to endless dole.
Ah, what a dusty answer gets the soul
When hot for certainties in this our life!—
In tragic hints here see what evermore
Moves dark as yonder midnight ocean's force,
Thundering like ramping hosts of warrior horse,
To throw that faint thin line upon the shore!

Dante Gabriel Rossetti (1828–1882)

*All Rossetti's sonnets, unlike his earlier "Pre-Raphaelite" poems,
employ ornate and highly decorated language and imagery. Words
and images are richly colored and suggestive rather than clear or
precise, and Rossetti's preference for a Latinate vocabulary gives
his verse a deliberate movement and a sense of weight and fullness
that, at their best, are very impressive. His belief in and practice of
what he called "fundamental brainwork" prevents his poetry from
becoming too vague, overly languid, or cloying, like the work of
the early Keats whom in some ways he so much resembled. Rossetti's
sonnets, however laden with gorgeous imagery and magnificent
language, are firmly structured in thought.*

FROM *The House of Life*

Lovesight

*Note the employment of the old courtly love tradition, in which
the lover's worship of the mistress becomes a kind of secular religion.*

The sestet shows Rossetti's frequent allegorical use of figures drawn from nature.

When do I see thee most, beloved one?
  When in the light the spirits of mine eyes
  Before thy face, their altar, solemnize
The worship of that Love through thee made known?
Or when in the dusk hours, (we two alone,)
  Close-kissed and eloquent of still replies
  Thy twilight-hidden glimmering visage lies,
And my soul only sees thy soul its own?

O love, my love! if I no more should see
Thyself, nor on the earth the shadow of thee,
  Nor image of thine eyes in any spring,—
How then should sound upon Life's darkening slope
The ground-whirl of the perished leaves of Hope,
  The wind of Death's imperishable wing?

Nuptial Sleep

Notorious in its time for inspiring Robert Buchanan's attack entitled "The Fleshly School of Poetry." Buchanan, a critic and himself a minor poet, accused Rossetti of extolling "fleshliness as the distinct and supreme end of poetic and pictorial art" and of preferring expression to thought, sound to sense, and body to soul. Rossetti contented himself with a dignified answer entitled "The Stealthy School of Criticism," defending "Nuptial Sleep" as one in a series, whose whole effect was not to show the body greater than the soul. He was, however, devastated by Buchanan's charge, and it seems to have been at least in part responsible for his deterioration in physical and mental health. Certainly Rossetti's voluptuous but precise imagery of sexual love ought to be both an example and a reproach to legions of young poets who find themselves reduced to the same overworked monosyllable in their efforts to convey this experience.

At length their long kiss severed, with sweet smart:
  And as the last slow sudden drops are shed

From sparkling eaves when all the storm has fled,
So singly flagged the pulses of each heart.
Their bosoms sundered, with the opening start
  Of married flowers to either side outspread
  From the knit stem; yet still their mouths, burnt red,
Fawned on each other where they lay apart.

Sleep sank them lower than the tide of dreams,
  And their dreams watched them sink, and slid away.
Slowly their souls swam up again, through gleams
  Of watered light and dull drowned waifs of day;
Till from some wonder of new woods and streams
    He woke, and wondered more: for there she lay.

Silent Noon

*A perfect example of Rossetti's own definition of a sonnet. See
"The Sonnet" (p. ii).*

Your hands lie open in the long fresh grass,—
  The finger-points look through like rosy blooms:
  Your eyes smile peace. The pasture gleams and glooms
'Neath billowing skies that scatter and amass.
All around our nest, far as the eye can pass,
  Are golden kingcup-fields with silver edge
  Where the cow-parsley skirts the hawthorn-hedge.
'T is visible silence, still as the hour-glass.

Deep in the sun-searched growths the dragon-fly
Hangs like a blue thread loosened from the sky:—
  So this wing'd hour is dropt to us from above.
Oh! clasp we to our hearts, for deathless dower,
This close-companioned inarticulate hour
  When twofold silence was the song of love.

Willowwood—I

I sat with Love upon a woodside well,
   Leaning across the water, I and he;
   Nor ever did he speak nor looked at me,
But touched his lute wherein was audible
The certain secret thing he had to tell:
   Only our mirrored eyes met silently
   In the low wave; and that sound came to be
The passionate voice I knew; and my tears fell.

And at their fall, his eyes beneath grew hers;
And with his foot and with his wing-feathers
   He swept the spring that watered my heart's drouth.
Then the dark ripples spread to waving hair,
And as I stooped, her own lips rising there
   Bubbled with brimming kisses at my mouth.

Without Her

What of her glass without her? The blank gray
   There where the pool is blind of the moon's face.
   Her dress without her? The tossed empty space
Of cloud-rack whence the moon has passed away.
Her paths without her? Day's appointed sway
   Usurped by desolate night. Her pillowed place
   Without her? Tears, ah me! for love's good grace
And cold forgetfulness of night or day.

What of the heart without her? Nay, poor heart,
   Of thee what word remains ere speech be still?
   A wayfarer by barren ways and chill,
Steep ways and weary, without her thou art,
Where the long cloud, the long wood's counterpart,
   Sheds doubled darkness up the labouring hill.

The Choice—III

Think thou and act; to-morrow thou shalt die.
  Outstretched in the sun's warmth upon the shore,
  Thou say'st: "Man's measured path is all gone o'er:
Up all his years, steeply, with strain and sigh,
Man clomb until he touched the truth; and I,
  Even I, am he whom it was destined for."
  How should this be? Art thou then so much more
Than they who sowed, that thou shouldst reap thereby?

Nay, come up hither. From this wave-washed mound
  Unto the furthest flood-brim look with me;
Then reach on with thy thought till it be drown'd.
  Miles and miles distant though the last line be,
And though thy soul sail leagues and leagues beyond,—
  Still, leagues beyond those leagues, there is more sea.

Soul's Beauty

*This sonnet and the one that follows, taken together, express the
essence of Rossetti's philosophy. Sensual love for him is not mere
"fleshly" enjoyment, as Buchanan charged, nor is it even communion with a particular beloved woman. Through bodily love
the soul is led to the ardent and mystical worship of Beauty herself.*

Under the arch of Life, where love and death,
  Terror and mystery, guard her shrine, I saw
  Beauty enthroned; and though her gaze struck awe,
I drew it in as simply as my breath.
Hers are the eyes which, over and beneath,
  The sky and sea bend on thee,—which can draw,
  By sea or sky or woman, to one law,
The allotted bondman of her palm and wreath.

This is that Lady Beauty, in whose praise
  Thy voice and hand shake still,—long known to thee

By flying hair and fluttering hem,—the beat
Following her daily of thy heart and feet,
How passionately and irretrievably,
In what fond flight, how many ways and days!

Body's Beauty

Of Adam's first wife, Lilith, it is told
(The witch he loved before the gift of Eve,)
That, ere the snake's, her sweet tongue could deceive,
And her enchanted hair was the first gold.
And still she sits, young while the earth is old,
And, subtly of herself contemplative,
Draws men to watch the bright web she can weave,
Till heart and body and life are in its hold.

The rose and poppy are her flowers; for where
Is he not found, O Lilith, whom shed scent
And soft-shed kisses and soft sleep shall snare?
Lo! as that youth's eyes burned at thine, so went
Thy spell through him, and left his straight neck bent
And round his heart one strangling golden hair.

A Superscription

Look in my face; my name is Might-have-been;
I am also called No-more, Too-late, Fare-well;
Unto thine ear I hold the dead-sea shell
Cast up thy Life's foam-fretted feet between:
Unto thine eyes the glass where that is seen
Which had Life's form and Love's, but by my spell
Is now a shaken shadow intolerable,
Of ultimate things unuttered the frail screen.

Mark me, how still I am! But should there dart
One moment through thy soul the soft surprise
Of that winged Peace which lulls the breath of sighs,—

Then shalt thou see me smile, and turn apart
Thy visage to mine ambush at thy heart
   Sleepless with cold commemorative eyes.

The One Hope

When vain desire at last and vain regret
   Go hand in hand to death, and all is vain,
   What shall assuage the unforgotten pain
And teach the unforgetful to forget?
Shall Peace be still a sunk stream long unmet,—
   Or may the soul at once in a green plain
   Stoop through the spray of some sweet life-fountain
And cull the dew-drenched flowering amulet?

Ah! when the wan soul in that golden air
   Between the scriptured petals softly blown
   Peers breathless for the gift of grace unknown,—
Ah! let none other alien spell soe'er
But only the one Hope's one name be there,—
   Not less nor more, but even that word alone.

Christina Rossetti (1830–1894)

Remember

*Compare this sonnet with Shakespeare's 71–"No longer mourn
for me when I am dead," (p. 45).*

Remember me when I am gone away,
   Gone far away into the silent land;
   When you can no more hold me by the hand,
Nor I half turn to go yet turning stay.
Remember me when no more day by day

You tell me of our future that you plann'd:
Only remember me; you understand
It will be late to counsel then or pray.
Yet if you should forget me for a while
And afterwards remember, do not grieve:
For if the darkness and corruption leave
A vestige of the thoughts that once I had,
Better by far you should forget and smile
Than that you should remember and be sad.

FROM *The Thread of Life*

1–"The irresponsive silence of the land"

Note the effective use of repetition in word and structure.

The irresponsive silence of the land,
The irresponsive sounding of the sea,
Speak both one message of one sense to me:—
Aloof, aloof, we stand aloof, so stand
Thou too aloof bound with the flawless band
Of inner solitude; we bind not thee;
But who from thy self-chain shall set thee free?
What heart shall touch thy heart? what hand thy hand?—
And I am sometimes proud and sometimes meek,
And sometimes I remember days of old
When fellowship seemed not so far to seek
And all the world and I seemed much less cold,
And at the rainbow's foot lay surely gold,
And hope felt strong and life itself not weak.

FROM *Monna Innominata*

6–"Trust me, I have not earned your dear rebuke"

*'Or puoi la quantitate
Comprender de l'amor che a te mi scalda.'*
                                        DANTE

'Non vo' che da tal nodo amor mi scioglia.'

PETRARCA

Trust me, I have not earned your dear rebuke,—
  I love, as you would have me, God the most;
  Would lose not Him, but you, must one be lost,
Nor with Lot's wife cast back a faithless look,
Unready to forego what I forsook;
  This say I, having counted up the cost,
  This, though I be the feeblest of God's host,
The sorriest sheep Christ shepherds with His crook.
Yet while I love my God the most, I deem
  That I can never love you overmuch;
  I love Him more so let me love you too;
  Yea, as I apprehend it, love is such
I cannot love you if I love not Him,
  I cannot love Him if I love not you.

13–"If I could trust mine own self . . ."

'E drizzeremo gli occhi al Primo Amore.'

DANTE

'Ma trovo peso non da le mie braccia.'

PETRARCA

If I could trust mine own self with your fate,
  Shall I not rather trust it in God's hand?
  Without Whose Will one lily doth not stand,
Nor sparrow fall at his appointed date;
  Who numbereth the innumerable sand,
Who weighs the wind and water with a weight,
To Whom the world is neither small nor great,
  Whose knowledge foreknew every plan we planned.
Searching my heart for all that touches you,
  I find there only love and love's goodwill
Helpless to help and impotent to do,
Of understanding dull, of sight most dim;
And therefore I commend you back to Him
  Whose love your love's capacity can fill.

14–"Youth gone, and beauty gone . . ."

'E la Sua Voluntade è nostra pace.'

DANTE

'Sol con questi pensier, con altre chiome.'

PETRARCA

Youth gone, and beauty gone if ever there
  Dwelt beauty in so poor a face as this;
  Youth gone and beauty, what remains of bliss?
I will not bind fresh roses in my hair,
To shame a cheek at best but little fair,—
  Leave youth his roses, who can bear a thorn,—
I will not seek for blossoms anywhere,
  Except such common flowers as blow with corn.
Youth gone and beauty gone, what doth remain?
The longing of a heart pent up forlorn,
  A silent heart whose silence loves and longs;
  The silence of a heart which sang its songs
While youth and beauty made a summer morn,
Silence of love that cannot sing again.

Rest

O earth, lie heavily upon her eyes;
  Seal her sweet eyes weary of watching, Earth;
  Lie close around her; leave no room for mirth
With its harsh laughter, nor for sound of sighs.
She hath no questions, she hath no replies,
  Hush'd in and curtain'd with a blessèd dearth
  Of all that irked her from the hour of birth;
With stillness that is almost Paradise.
Darkness more clear than noonday holdeth her,
  Silence more musical than any song;
Even her very heart has ceased to stir:
Until the morning of Eternity

Her rest shall not begin nor end, but be;
  And when she wakes she will not think it long.

Alfred Austin (1835–1913)

A Sleepless Night

A typical Victorian sonnet, in which the poet's personal feeling of isolation is made the basis for philosophical implications and inferences about the universe.

Within the hollow silence of the night
I lay awake and listened. I could hear
Planet with punctual planet chiming clear,
And unto star star cadencing aright.
Nor these alone: cloistered from deafening sight,
All things that are made music to my ear:
Hushed woods, dumb caves, and many a soundless mere,
With Arctic mains in rigid sleep locked tight.
But ever with this chant from shore and sea,
From singing constellation, humming thought,
And Life through Time's stops blowing variously,
A melancholy undertone was wrought;
And from its boundless prison-house I caught
The awful wail of lone Eternity.

Samuel Butler (1835–1902)

A Prayer

A refreshing reversal of conventional Victorian piety by the author of a scathing attack on it, The Way of All Flesh. *Note the ironic use of scriptural phraseology, particularly Psalm 19:12.*

Searcher of souls, you who in heaven abide,
To whom the secrets of all hearts are open,
Though I do lie to all the world beside,
From me to thee no falsehood shall be spoken.
Cleanse me not, Lord, I say, from secret sin
But from those faults which he who runs can see.
'Tis these that torture me, O Lord, begin
With these and let the hidden vices be;
If you must cleanse these too, at any rate
Deal with the seen sins first, 'tis only reason,
They being so gross, to let the others wait
The leisure of some more convenient season;
    And cleanse not all even then, leave me a few.
    I would not be—not quite—so pure as you.

Algernon Charles Swinburne (*1837–1901*)

On the Russian Persecution of the Jews

*A passionately rhetorical onslaught against not Christ but Christians,
by the* enfant terrible *of his generation. The Christ of this sonnet
is a different figure from the "pale Galilean" of Swinburne's more
famous "Hymn to Proserpine." Compare the sonnet's overemphatic diction and obtrusive use of sound devices with Milton's
sonnet on the Piedmont massacre (p. 60).*

O son of man, by lying tongues adored,
    By slaughterous hands of slaves with feet red-shod
    In carnage deep as ever Christian trod
Profaned with prayer and sacrifice abhorred
And incense from the trembling tyrant's horde,
    Brute worshippers of wielders of the rod,
    Most murderous even of all that call thee God,
Most treacherous even that ever called thee Lord;
Face loved of little children long ago,

Head hated of the priests and rulers then,
   If thou see this, or hear these hounds of thine
   Run ravening as the Gadarean swine,
Say, was not this thy Passion to foreknow
In death's worst hour the works of Christian men?

Wilfrid Scawen Blunt (1840–1922)

Blunt's sonnets are a salutary reminder of the error of insisting on a pedantic regularity of rhyme scheme and structure. The best of them are irregular, sometimes a mixture of the Italian and the Shakespearean forms, sometimes variations on one or the other basic pattern, sometimes abandoning any formal scheme for an apparently hit or miss grab-bag of rhymes. They succeed nonetheless by virtue of an unusual energy, whether Blunt is expostulating with Time and Death or remembering youth and love. Their tonic quality is rare in this period.

St. Valentine's Day

To-day, all day, I rode upon the down,
With hounds and horsemen, a brave company,
On this side in its glory lay the sea,
On that the Sussex weald, a sea of brown.
The wind was light, and brightly the sun shone,
And still we gallop'd on from gorse to gorse:
And once, when check'd, a thrush sang, and my horse
Prick'd his quick ears as to a sound unknown.
   I knew the Spring was come. I knew it even
Better than all by this, that through my chase
In bush and stone and hill and sea and heaven
I seem'd to see and follow still your face.
Your face my quarry was. For it I rode,
My horse a thing of wings, myself a god.

On the Shortness of Time

If I could live without the thought of death,
Forgetful of Time's waste, the soul's decay,
I would not ask for other joy than breath,
With light and sound of birds and the sun's ray.
I could sit on untroubled day by day
Watching the grass grow, and the wild flowers range
From blue to yellow and from red to grey
In natural sequence as the seasons change.
I could afford to wait, but for the hurt
Of this dull tick of time which chides my ear.
But now I dare not sit with loins ungirt
And staff unlifted, for death stands too near.
I must be up and doing—ay, each minute.
The grave gives time for rest when we are in it.

"When I hear laughter . . ."

When I hear laughter from a tavern door,
When I see crowds agape and in the rain
Watching on tiptoe and with stifled roar
To see a rocket fired or a bull slain,
When misers handle gold, when orators
Touch strong men's hearts with glory till they weep,
When cities deck their streets for barren wars
Which have laid waste their youth, and when I keep
Calmly the count of my own life and see
On what poor stuff my manhood's dreams were fed
Till I too learned what dole of vanity
Will serve a human soul for daily bread,
—Then I remember that I once was young
And lived with Esther the world's gods among.

The Two Highwaymen

I long have had a quarrel set with Time,
Because he robbed me. Every day of life
Was wrested from me after bitter strife;
I never yet could see the sun go down
But I was angry in my heart, nor hear
The leaves fall in the wind without a tear
Over the dying summer. I have known
No truce with Time nor Time's accomplice Death.
The fair world is the witness of a crime
Repeated every hour. For life and breath
Are sweet to all who live; and bitterly
The voices of these robbers of the heath
Sound in each ear and chill the passer-by.
—What have we done to thee, thou monstrous Time?
What have we done to Death that we must die?

John Addington Symonds (1840–1893)

Venetian Sunrise

Remarkable for its impressionist-painting-like quality,
all light and color.

How often have I now outwatched the night
   Alone in this grey chamber toward the sea
   Turning its deep-arcaded balcony!
Round yonder sharp acanthus-leaves the light
Comes stealing, red at first, then golden bright;
   Till when the day-god in his strength and glee
   Springs from the orient flood victoriously,
Each cusp is tipped and tongued with quivering white.

The islands that were blots of purple bloom,
  Now tremble in soft liquid luminous haze,
  Uplifted from the sea-floor to the skies;
And dim discerned erewhile through roseate gloom,
  A score of sails now stud the waterways,
  Ruffling like swans afloat from paradise.

Thomas Hardy (1840–1928)

Hap

An early sonnet that sounds Hardy's characteristic note and theme.
The "purblind Doomsters" who play at dice with the lives of men
are a constant feature of his verse and fiction alike. Note the
ironic use of pilgrimage, *a common image for the Christian journey,*
as in Pilgrim's Progress, *through the "wilderness of this world"*
to the Celestial City.

If but some vengeful god would call to me
From up the sky, and laugh: "Thou suffering thing,
Know that thy sorrow is my ecstasy,
That thy love's loss is my hate's profiting!"

Then would I bear it, clench myself, and die,
Steeled by the sense of ire unmerited;
Half-eased in that a Powerfuller than I
Had willed and meted me the tears I shed.

But not so. How arrives it joy lies slain,
And why unblooms the best hope ever sown?
—Crass Casualty obstructs the sun and rain,
And dicing Time for gladness casts a moan. . . .
These purblind Doomsters had as readily strown
Blisses about my pilgrimage as pain.

At a Lunar Eclipse

An effective dramatization of Hardy's central perception: the contrast between men's vision of their lives and the "small . . . shade" thrown by "immense Mortality" into the indifferent immensities of the cosmos. Compare Hardy's use of the moon with that of earlier poets who still could view her as Cynthia, the goddess who had loved a mortal and would therefore "feel a lover's case," as in Sidney's sonnet (p. 24). It is this change in attitude and outlook that Poe is lamenting in "To Science."

Thy shadow, Earth, from Pole to Central Sea,
Now steals along upon the Moon's meek shine
In even monochrome and curving line
Of imperturbable serenity.

How shall I link such sun-cast symmetry
With the torn troubled form I know as thine,
That profile, placid as a brow divine,
With continents of moil and misery?

And can immense Mortality but throw
So small a shade, and Heaven's high human scheme
Be hemmed within the coasts yon arc implies?

Is such the stellar gauge of earthly show,
Nation at war with nation, brains that teem,
Heroes, and women fairer than the skies?

Zermatt

Here, as in "At a Lunar Eclipse" Hardy takes a topical subject and through it dramatizes the gulf between human lives, human history, and the oblivious universe. Note the biblical references. Hardy was steeped in the stories, the symbolism, and the phraseology of the

Bible, both Old and New Testaments; and he uses all three again and again with great dramatic effect.

> Thirty-two years since, up against the sun,
> Seven shapes, thin atomies to lower sight,
> Labouringly leapt and gained thy gabled height,
> And four lives paid for what the seven had won.
>
> They were the first by whom the deed was done,
> And when I look at thee, my mind takes flight
> To that day's tragic feat of manly might,
> As though, till then, of history thou hadst none.
>
> Yet ages ere men topped thee, late and soon
> Thou didst behold the planets lift and lower;
> Saw'st, maybe, Joshua's pausing sun and moon,
> And the betokening sky when Cæsar's power
> Approached its bloody end; yea, even that Noon
> When darkness filled the earth till the ninth hour.

In the Cemetery

From Satires of Circumstance, *a volume of poems published in 1914. This sonnet is particularly effective in its picture of the indifference and cruelty displayed by the grieving mothers toward their fellows, and the almost godlike comprehension and cool compassion shown by the "man of the cemetery." Note the handling of dialogue and the deflating image of the eighth line.*

> "You see those mothers squabbling there?"
> Remarks the man of the cemetery.
> "One says in tears, ' 'Tis mine lies here!'
> Another, 'Nay, mine, you Pharisee!'
> Another, 'How dare you move my flowers
> And put your own on this grave of ours!'
> But all their children were laid therein
> At different times, like sprats in a tin.
> "And then the main drain had to cross,

And we moved the lot some nights ago,
And packed them away in the general foss
With hundreds more. But their folks don't know,
And as well cry over a new-laid drain
As anything else, to ease your pain!"

At the Altar Rail

Also from Satires of Circumstance. *Note the odd division of parts and the rhyme scheme.*

"My bride is not coming, alas!" says the groom,
And the telegram shakes in his hand. "I own
It was hurried! We met at a dancing-room
When I went to the Cattle-Show alone,
And then, next night, where the Fountain leaps,
And the Street of the Quarter-Circle sweeps.

"Ay, she won me to ask her to be my wife—
'Twas foolish perhaps!—to forsake the ways
Of the flaring town for a farmer's life.
She agreed. And we fixed it. Now she says:
'It's sweet of you, dear, to prepare me a nest,
But a swift, short, gay life suits me best.
What I really am you have never gleaned;
I had eaten the apple ere you were weaned.' "

She, to Him

A familiar theme presented from the woman's point of view—a rare occurrence. Note the figure in line 10 and compare it with the use of the same symbolism in Hardy's novel Tess of the D'Urbervilles, *at the time of Tess' seduction by Alec D'Urberville.*

When you shall see me in the toils of Time,
My lauded beauties carried off from me,

My eyes no longer stars as in their prime,
My name forgot of Maiden Fair and Free;

When, in your being, heart concedes to mind,
And judgment, though you scarce its process know,
Recalls the excellencies I once enshrined,
And you are irked that they have withered so:

Remembering mine the loss is, not the blame,
That Sportsman Time but rears his brood to kill,
Knowing me in my soul the very same—
One who would die to spare you touch of ill!—
Will you not grant to old affection's claim
The hand of friendship down Life's sunless hill?

The Pity Of It

*Only Hardy, perhaps, could have felt and written like this
at this time, during World War I.*

I walked in loamy Wessex lanes, afar
From rail-track and from highway, and I heard
In field and farmstead many an ancient word
Of local lineage like "Thu bist," "Er war,"

"Ich woll," "Er sholl," and by-talk similar,
Nigh as they speak who in this month's moon gird
At England's very loins, thereunto spurred
By gangs whose glory threats and slaughters are.

Then seemed a Heart crying: "Whosoever they be
At root and bottom of this, who flung this flame
Between kin folk kin tongued even as are we,

"Sinister, ugly, lurid, be their fame;
May their familiars grow to shun their name,
And their brood perish everlastingly."

Andrew Lang (1844–1912)

The Odyssey

*Note Lang's implication that the great literature of the past is both
a refuge from and an antidote to that of his own time. Compare
this attitude with that expressed by Keats in his sonnet on
Chapman's Homer (p. 84). The freshness, the eagerness, the
exhilaration and wonder of the romantic poet have become the
weariness and sense of degeneration of the Victorian.*

> As one that for a weary space has lain
>   Lull'd by the song of Circe and her wine
>   In gardens near the pale of Proserpine,
> Where that Ææan isle forgets the main,
> And only the low lutes of love complain,
>   And only shadows of wan lovers pine—
>   As such an one were glad to know the brine
> Salt on his lips, and the large air again,—
> So gladly, from the songs of modern speech
>   Men turn, and see the stars, and feel the free
>   Shrill wind beyond the close of heavy flowers,
>   And through the music of the languid hours
> They hear like Ocean on the western beach
>   The surge and thunder of the Odyssey.

Robert Bridges (1844–1889)

23–"O weary pilgrims . . ."

O weary pilgrims, chanting of your woe,
That turn your eyes to all the peaks that shine,
Hailing in each the citadel divine
The which ye thought to have enter'd long ago;
Until at length your feeble steps and slow
Falter upon the threshold of the shrine,
And your hearts overburden'd doubt in fine
Whether it be Jerusalem or no:

  Dishearten'd pilgrims, I am one of you;
For, having worshipp'd many a barren face,
I scarce now greet the goal I journey'd to:
I stand a pagan in the holy place;
Beneath the lamp of truth I am found untrue,
And question with the God that I embrace.

35–"All earthly beauty hath one cause and proof"

All earthly beauty hath one cause and proof,
To lead the pilgrim soul to beauty above:
Yet lieth the greater bliss so far aloof,
That few there be are wean'd from earthly love.
  Joy's ladder it is, reaching from home to home,
The best of all the work that all was good;
Whereof 'twas writ the angels aye upclomb,
Down sped, and at the top the Lord God stood.

  But I my time abuse, my eyes by day
Center'd on thee, by night my heart on fire—

Letting my number'd moments run away—
Nor e'en 'twixt night and day to heaven aspire:
   So true it is that what the eye seeth not
But slow is loved, and loved is soon forgot.

Gerard Manley Hopkins (1844–1889)

31–God's Grandeur

The first two lines present, by verbs and figures of power in action, the God who created and who inspires the world of nature. Abruptly the figure changes to the more elusive "greatness, like the ooze of oil/Crushed." From his letters, we know that Hopkins wrote pressed *before revising the word to the much stronger* crushed. *The oil—much misunderstood by commentators on the poem—is olive oil, produced quite literally by pressing or "crushing" olives. The central contrast of the first four lines is thus a "grandeur" or a "greatness" revealed first in action, then in passion; first in doing, then in suffering. God's grandeur "flames out" in the world. But the olives must be crushed if their oil is to "gather to a greatness." And the crushing of the olives for the oil is linked to the flaming, shining Holy Ghost, charging the whole world with power. Indeed, in the Catholic sacraments of Baptism and Confirmation, Chrism, a consecrated mixture of olive oil and balm, is applied to the forehead of the worshipper to symbolize the coming of the Holy Ghost.*

The link is not as yet developed. The poet turns to the theme of man's indifference to God's presence and His insistent demands on the spirit—His "rod." Like Wordsworth earlier, Hopkins feels even more strongly that men have "seared," laid over with ashes, the living freshness of nature, and have insulated their own sensibilities against the Divine presence, as a shod foot is insulated against contact with earth. The last four lines of the octave are an indictment of the modern world of industry and commerce; but the great contrasted yet connected images of the first four lines still wait, as it were, for the word that shall fuse them into one meaning of intense and concentrated power.

In the sestet, action and passion, matter and spirit, the world of Nature created by God and the world of industry created by man, the sinful world and the world redeemed, man and God, are reconciled. And since Hopkins, unlike the earlier romantic poet, was neither pagan nor pantheist, it is of the Christian God in His Three Persons that he speaks. The "dearest" freshness of nature is not only a freshness to be treasured; it is dearest in the English sense of expensive, bought at a great price. It was bought, in fact, by God Himself, who suffered and died to redeem the fallen world. "The last lights off the black West" invites us to remember the darkness that covered the whole land until the ninth hour at the Crucifixion (Mark 15:33); the morning that springs eastward is as surely "the dayspring from on High" (Luke 1:78) who rose like the sun on the first Easter morning. And the Christ who endured crucifixion and triumphed at the Resurrection underwent also the Agony in the Garden—the Garden of Gethsemane on the Mount of Olives. The olives are crushed for their oil, the oil of man's nourishment, the oil of anointment and consecration. And Christ was literally crushed at Gethsemane and on the cross for the sins of men. The Holy Ghost flames and shines in a world bought by the suffering, the crushing of Christ, a world forever redeemed by God from what man's sin had made of it. In the last lines the original image of flame, the Pentecostal tongues of fire, is converted into its companion figure of the dove, brooding over the "bent" world: the world that is both crooked—bent from its true nature and function—and bent under the burden of sin. And since Christianity sees spirit and matter as inseparably intermingled and God as involved with the world of nature, of history, of men, Hopkins' Holy Ghost is both flesh-and-blood bird, warm and brooding, and a spirit "with ah! bright wings."

> The world is charged with the grandeur of God.
>   It will flame out, like shining from shook foil;
>   It gathers to a greatness, like the ooze of oil
> Crushed. Why do men then now not reck his rod?
> Generations have trod, have trod, have trod;
>   And all is seared with trade; bleared, smeared with toil;

And wears man's smudge and shares man's smell: the soil
Is bare now, nor can foot feel, being shod.

And for all this, nature is never spent;
   There lives the dearest freshness deep down things;
And though the last lights off the black West went
   Oh, morning, at the brown brink eastward, springs—
Because the Holy Ghost over the bent
   World broods with warm breast and with ah! bright wings.

32–The Starlight Night

*In his early nature sonnets, Hopkins uses his sensuous appreciation
of the natural world for purposes of Christian parable. Here the
Christian is bidden to "buy" the bright beauty of the world with
"Prayer, patience, alms, vows," the world and the soul having
already been bought by Christ. Note the poet's use of compound
words, and particularly the pun in line 10: "May-mess," the fruit
tree blossoms, are the food of Christian communion, the mass (cf.
French* messe). *The sonnet is an extreme instance of Hopkins'
abrupt, exclamatory style.*

Look at the stars! look, look up at the skies!
   O look at all the fire-folk sitting in the air!
   The bright boroughs, the circle-citadels there!
Down in dim woods the diamond delves! the elves'-eyes!
The grey lawns cold where gold, where quickgold lies!
   Wind-beat whitebeam! airy abeles set on a flare!
   Flake-doves sent floating forth at a farmyard scare!—
Ah well! it is all a purchase, all is a prize.

Buy then! bid then!—What?—Prayer, patience, alms, vows.
Look, look: a May-mess, like on orchard boughs!
   Look! March-bloom, like on mealed-with-yellow sallows!
These are indeed the barn; withindoors house
The shocks. This piece-bright paling shuts the spouse
   Christ home, Christ and his mother and all his hallows.

33-Spring

*The spring of the year with all its "juice" and joy reminds the poet
of man's original unfallen state and of the innocence of early youth
before the world and the soul had grown "sour with sinning."
Note how the piercing beauty of the thrush's song, "rinsing" and
"wringing" the ear also strikes the eye "like lightnings"—a
combination of aural and visual imagery.*

Nothing is so beautiful as Spring—
　　When weeds, in wheels, shoot long and lovely and lush;
　　Thrush's eggs look little low heavens, and thrush
Through the echoing timber does so rinse and wring
The ear, it strikes like lightnings to hear him sing;
　　The glassy peartree leaves and blooms, they brush
　　The descending blue; that blue is all in a rush
With richness; the racing lambs too have fair their fling.

What is all this juice and all this joy?
　　A strain of the earth's sweet being in the beginning
In Eden garden.—Have, get, before it cloy,

　　Before it cloud, Christ, lord, and sour with sinning,
Innocent mind and Mayday in girl and boy,
　　Most, O maid's child, thy choice and worthy the winning.

36-The Windhover

*The rhythms and movement of this sonnet directly describe and
imitate the falcon in his easy mastery of the kingdom of air. Note
the pun in line 10 where* buckle *means both "fasten together" and
"crumble." "Brute beauty and valour and act" come together in
the falcon, symbol of physical and active power in the natural
world. But the spiritual mastery of Christ, chevalier of the kingdom
of passion, sacrifice, and suffering, is "a billion/Times told
lovelier, more dangerous."*

To Christ our Lord

I caught this morning morning's minion, king-
  dom of daylight's dauphin, dapple-dawn-drawn Falcon, in
    his riding
Of the rolling level underneath him steady air, and striding
High there, how he rung upon the rein of a wimpling wing
In his ecstasy! then off, off forth on swing,
  As a skate's heel sweeps smooth on a bow-bend: the hurl and
    gliding
Rebuffed the big wind. My heart in hiding
Stirred for a bird,—the achieve of, the mastery of the thing!

Brute beauty and valour and act, oh, air, pride, plume, here
  Buckle! AND the fire that breaks from thee then, a billion
Times told lovelier, more dangerous, O my chevalier!

No wonder of it: shéer plód makes plough down sillion
Shine, and blue-bleak embers, ah my dear,
  Fall, gall themselves, and gash gold-vermilion.

4—*wimpling:* rippling
5—*rung upon the rein:* like a horse circling around its trainer at the end of a long rein.
7—*in hiding:* dedicated to Christ, to whom the poem is dedicated and who is "my chevalier!" in line 11 and "ah my dear" in line 13.
11—*sillion:* furrow

38–Hurrahing in Harvest

Here the whole world is seen as theophany, the visible manifestation of Christ.

Summer ends now; now, barbarous in beauty, the stooks rise
Around; up above, what wind-walks! what lovely behaviour
Of silk-sack clouds! has wilder, wilful-wavier
Meal-drift moulded ever and melted across skies?

I walk, I lift up, I lift up heart, eyes,
Down all that glory in the heavens to glean our Saviour;

And, éyes, heárt, what looks, what lips yet gave you a
Rapturous love's greeting of realer, of rounder replies?

And the azurous hung hills are his world-wielding shoulder
Majestic—as a stallion stalwart, very-violet-sweet!—
These things, these things were here and but the beholder
Wanting; which two when they once meet,
The heart rears wings bold and bolder
And hurls for him, O half hurls earth for him off under his
feet.

39–The Caged Skylark

As a dare-gale skylark scanted in a dull cage
  Man's mounting spirit in his bone-house, mean house,
    dwells—
  That bird beyond the remembering his free fells;
This in drudgery, day-labouring-out life's age.

Though aloft on turf or perch or poor low stage,
  Both sing sometímes the sweetest, sweetest spells,
  Yet both droop deadly sómetimes in their cells
Or wring their barriers in bursts of fear or rage.

Not that the sweet-fowl, song-fowl, needs no rest—
Why, hear him, hear him babble and drop down to his nest,
  But his own nest, wild nest, no prison.

Man's spirit will be flesh-bound when found at best,
But uncumberèd: meadow-down is not distressed
  For a rainbow footing it nor he for his bónes rísen.

53–Felix Randal

*Note how the long, heavily accented line permits the poet an
almost discursive, conversational style and then, in the last three
lines, a resounding rhetorical conclusion.*

Felix Randal the farrier, O is he dead then? my duty all ended,
Who have watched his mould of man, big-boned and hardy-
handsome
Pining, pining, till time when reason rambled in it and some
Fatal four disorders, fleshed there, all contended?

Sickness broke him. Impatient, he cursed at first, but mended
Being anointed and all; though a heavenlier heart began some
Months earlier, since I had our sweet reprieve and ransom
Tendered to him. Ah well, God rest him all road ever he
offended!

This seeing the sick endears them to us, us too it endears.
My tongue had taught thee comfort, touch had quenched thy
tears,
Thy tears that touched my heart, child, Felix, poor Felix
Randal;

How far from then forethought of, all thy more boisterous
years,
When thou at the random grim forge, powerful amidst peers,
Didst fettle for the great grey drayhorse his bright and battering
sandal!

57-"As kingfishers catch fire . . ."

*A fine example of the influence on Hopkins of Duns Scotus, the
scholastic philosopher whose "principle of individuation" differed
from Thomism, the system taught by Jesuit theologians. According
to Scotus,* haecceitas *("this-ness") is the specific nature of a thing,
its active principle, shown in its function; and it is the real relation
between the creature and God. Hopkins puts the doctrine succinctly
in the last line of the octave: "Crying* What I do is me: for that I
came." *According to Hopkins' critic, W. H. Gardner, we see in this
sonnet "the most complete and successful union of the poet and
the Scotist . . . individual substances, according to the metaphysical
richness of their being, make up one vast hierarchy with God*

as their summit." [1] *Note especially the complicated and effective patterns of sound in lines 3–4.*

> As kingfishers catch fire, dragonflies draw flame;
>   As tumbled over rim in roundy wells
>   Stones ring; like each tucked string tells, each hung bell's
> Bow swung finds tongue to fling out broad its name;
> Each mortal thing does one thing and the same:
>   Deals out that being indoors each one dwells;
>   Selves—goes itself; *myself* it speaks and spells,
> Crying *What I do is me: for that I came.*
>
> Í say more: the just man justices;
>   Keeps gráce: thát keeps all his goings graces;
> Acts in God's eye what in God's eye he is—
>   Chríst. For Christ plays in ten thousand places,
> Lovely in limbs, and lovely in eyes not his
>   To the Father through the features of men's faces.

64–(Carrion Comfort)

One of the so-called "terrible sonnets" in which Hopkins records some bitter spiritual distress that afflicted him. The "carrion comfort, Despair," on whom the poet refuses to feast, becomes abruptly in the second quatrain a monster threatening to feast on him, in images that seem to come from a nightmare fairy tale. In the sestet, though the urgent tone does not diminish, the perspective shifts from immediate present to past. The poet, looking back on "that year/Of now done darkness" recognizes with a gasp whom he has contended with: "(my God!) my God."

> Not, I'll not, carrion comfort, Despair, not feast on thee;
> Not untwist—slack they may be—these last strands of man
> In me ór, most weary, cry *I can no more.* I can;
> Can something, hope, wish day come, not choose not to be.

[1] *Gerard Manley Hopkins* (London, 1944), p. 27.

But ah, but O thou terrible, why wouldst thou rude on me
Thy wring-world right foot rock? lay a lionlimb against me?
    scan
With darksome devouring eyes my bruisèd bones? and fan,
O in turns of tempest, me heaped there; me frantic to avoid
    thee and flee?

Why? That my chaff might fly; my grain lie, sheer and clear.
Nay in all that toil, that coil, since (seems) I kissed the rod,
Hand rather, my heart lo! lapped strength, stole joy, would
    laugh, chéer.
Cheer whom though? The hero whose heaven-handling flung
    me, fóot tród
Me? or me that fought him? O which one? is it each one?
    That night, that year
Of now done darkness I wretch lay wrestling with (my God!)
    my God.

65–"No worst, there is none . . ."

No worst, there is none. Pitched past pitch of grief,
More pangs will, schooled at forepangs, wilder wring.
Comforter, where, where is your comforting?
Mary, mother of us, where is your relief?
My cries heave, herds-long; huddle in a main, a chief-
woe, world-sorrow; on an age-old anvil wince and sing—
Then lull, then leave off. Fury had shrieked 'No ling-
ering! Let me be fell: force I must be brief'.
O the mind, mind has mountains; cliffs of fall
Frightful, sheer, no-man-fathomed. Hold them cheap
May who ne'er hung there. Nor does long our small
Durance deal with that steep or deep. Here! creep,
Wretch, under a comfort serves in a whirlwind: all
Life death does end and each day dies with sleep.

67–"I wake and feel the fell of dark . . ."

Fell is used in two distinct though related meanings, the noun meaning the skin of a wild beast, and the adjective meaning "evil." The effect is to make the poet's spiritual agony an almost tangible experience. Note the vivid, homely, physical images of the sestet.

I wake and feel the fell of dark, not day.
What hours, O what black hoürs we have spent
This night! what sights you, heart, saw; ways you went!
And more must, in yet longer light's delay.

With witness I speak this. But where I say
Hours I mean years, mean life. And my lament
Is cries countless, cries like dead letters sent
To dearest him that lives alas! away.

I am gall, I am heartburn. God's most deep decree
Bitter would have me taste: my taste was me;
Bones built in me, flesh filled, blood brimmed the curse.

Selfyeast of spirit a dull dough sours. I see
The lost are like this, and their scourge to be
As I am mine, their sweating selves; but worse.

74–"Thou art indeed just, Lord . . ."

Justus quidem tu es, Domine, si disputem tecum; verumtamen justa loquar ad te: Quare via impiorum prosperatur? &c.

Thou art indeed just, Lord, if I contend
With thee; but, sir, so what I plead is just.
Why do sinners' ways prosper? and why must
Disappointment all I endeavour end?

Wert thou my enemy, O thou my friend,
How wouldst thou worse, I wonder, than thou dost
Defeat, thwart me? Oh, the sots and thralls of lust
Do in spare hours more thrive than I that spend,

Sir, life upon thy cause. See, banks and brakes
Now, leavèd how thick! lacèd they are again
With fretty chervil, look, and fresh wind shakes

Them; birds build—but not I build; no, but strain,
Time's eunuch, and not breed one work that wakes.
Mine, O thou lord of life, send my roots rain.

Eugene Lee-Hamilton (1845–1907)

"Oh, bless the law . . ."

A typical Victorian sonnet.

Oh, bless the law that veils the Future's face;
For who could smile into a baby's eyes,
Or bear the beauty of the evening skies,
If he could see what cometh on apace?
The ticking of the death-watch would replace
The baby's prattle, for the over-wise;
The breeze's murmur would become the cries
Of stormy petrels where the breakers race.
We live as moves the walker in his sleep,
Who walks because he sees not the abyss
His feet are skirting as he goes his way:
If we could see the morrow from the steep
Of our security, the soul would miss
Its footing, and fall headlong from today.

Idle Charon

The loss of religious faith is here, as so often in this period,
linked to the loss of the old world of the imagination.

The shores of Styx are lone for evermore,
    And not one shadowy form upon the steep
    Looms through the dusk, far as the eye can sweep,
To call the ferry over as of yore;
But tintless rushes all about the shore
    Have hemmed the old boat in, where, locked in sleep,
    Hoar-bearded Charon lies; while pale weeds creep
With tightening grasp all round the unused oar.

For in the world of Life strange rumours run
    That now the soul departs not with the breath,
But that the Body and the Soul are one;
    And in the loved one's mouth, now, after death,
The widow puts no obol, nor the son,
    To pay the ferry in the world beneath.

Alice Meynell (1847–1922)

Renouncement

I must not think of thee; and, tired yet strong,
    I shun the love that lurks in all delight—
    The love of thee—and in the blue Heaven's height,
And in the dearest passage of a song.
Oh, just beyond the sweetest thoughts that throng
    This breast, the thought of thee waits hidden yet bright;
    But it must never, never come in sight;
I must stop short of thee the whole day long.

But when sleep comes to close each difficult day,
    When night gives pause to the long watch I keep,
    And all my bonds I needs must loose apart,
Must doff my will as raiment laid away,—
    With the first dream that comes with the first sleep
    I run, I run, I am gathered to thy heart.

Edmund Gosse (1849–1928)

The Fear of Death

In its very minor way, this sonnet sounds the same note Arnold struck in "Dover Beach," that central document of the Victorian age. Only personal relationships are left to rely on in the absence of all other certainties. The dread of death, the loss of the living present of beauty and love, has become not sharper than in the past but more pathetic, for there is now neither hope of immortality nor the consolation of living in fame or memory. The characteristic sense of isolation and loneliness in the period comes from this feeling of having been cut off from both past and future and condemned to live like Robinson Crusoe on the all-but-desert island of the present.

Last night I woke and found between us drawn—
Between us, where no mortal fear may creep—
The vision of Death dividing us in sleep;
And suddenly I thought, Ere light shall dawn
Some day,—the substance, not the shadow, of Death
Shall cleave us like a sword. The vision passed,
But all its new-born horror held me fast,
And till day broke I listened for your breath.
Some day to wake, and find that coloured skies,
And pipings in the woods, and petals wet,
Are things for aching memory to forget;
And that your living hands and mouth and eyes

Are part of all the world's old histories!—
Dear God! a little longer, ah, not yet!

William Ernest Henley (1849–1903)

Apparition

The "apparition" of the poem is Henley's close friend Robert Louis
Stevenson. This kind of individual portrait of someone personally
well-known to the writer is something new in the sonnet. The poem
is neither eulogy, elegy, nor summons, like earlier sonnets addressed
to individuals, but a portrait of both outer and inner man. Note
the mixture of close observation and psychological analysis, the use
of literary comparisons, and the sly touch of humor at the end.

Thin-legged, thin-chested, slight unspeakably,
Neat-footed and weak-fingered: in his face—
Lean, large-boned, curved of beak, and touched with race,
Bold-lipped, rich-tinted, mutable as the sea,
The brown eyes radiant with vivacity—
There shines a brilliant and romantic grace,
A spirit intense and rare, with trace on trace
Of passion and impudence and energy.
Valiant in velvet, light in ragged luck,
Most vain, most generous, sternly critical,
Buffoon and poet, lover and sensualist:
A deal of Ariel, just a streak of Puck,
Much of Antony, of Hamlet most of all,
And something of the Shorter-Catechist.

Before

Another instance of the widening of subject bounds to include
experiences hitherto not the province of the sonnet. The increasing

emphasis on individual particulars of personal experience rather than some more generalized treatment or a more conventional topic appears at this time and continues in the twentieth century.

Behold me waiting—waiting for the knife.
A little while, and at a leap I storm
The thick, sweet mystery of chloroform,
The drunken dark, the little death-in-life.
The gods are good to me—I have no wife,
No innocent child, to think of as I near
The fateful minute; nothing all-too dear
Unmans me for my bout of passive strife.
Yet I am tremulous and a trifle sick,
And, face to face with chance, I shrink a little;
My hopes are strong, my will is something weak.
Here comes the basket? Thank you. I am ready.
But, gentlemen my porters, life is brittle;
You carry Cæsar and his fortunes—steady!

James Kenneth Stephen (1859–1892)

"Two voices are there . . ."

A fine parody of Wordsworth's style, combining satire with tribute.

Two voices are there: one is of the deep;
It learns the storm-cloud's thunderous melody,
Now roars, now murmurs with the changing sea,
Now bird-like pipes, now closes soft in sleep;
And one is of an old half-witted sheep
Which bleats articulate monotony,
And indicates that two and one are three,
That grass is green, lakes damp, and mountains steep:
And, Wordsworth, both are thine; at certain times,
Forth from the heart of thy melodious rimes

The form and pressure of high thoughts will burst;
At other times—good Lord! I'd rather be
Quite unacquainted with the A. B. C.
Than write such hopeless rubbish as thy worst.

Oscar Wilde (1856–1900)

Wilde's sonnets show a side of his many-faceted temperament very different from those displayed in the comedies, in Salome, or even in "The Ballad of Reading Gaol," which are better known. Few poems of the period more poignantly reveal the emotional pull still exerted by Christ, if not Christianity, and the sense of sin by which these reluctant unbelievers were tortured. Wilde's Christ is not Swinburne's "pale Galilean," enemy of life and love.

On Hearing the "Dies Irae" Sung in the Sistine Chapel

This sonnet speaks of a Christ who is a lover, like the poet himself, of the beauty of the world, one who would surely repudiate the punitive aspect in which the Church presents Him. Note how easily and effectively Wilde uses natural imagery to recall Christian story and symbol.

Nay, Lord, not thus! white lilies in the spring,
Sad olive-groves, or silver-breasted dove,
Teach me more clearly of Thy life and love
Than terrors of red flame and thundering.
The hillside vines dear memories of Thee bring:
A bird at evening flying to its nest
Tells me of One who had no place of rest:
I think it is of Thee the sparrows sing.
Come rather on some autumn afternoon,
When red and brown are burnished on the leaves,
And the fields echo to the gleaner's song,

Come when the splendid fulness of the moon
Looks down upon the rows of golden sheaves,
And reap Thy harvest: we have waited long.

E Tenebris

A personal plea (the title means "Out of the shades"), its Christ
even more explicitly the friend of sinners and the comforter of the
heavy-laden heart. Again Wilde uses metaphors drawn from
biblical episodes. The voice of the unbeliever that speaks in lines
9–11 refers to Elijah's victory over the priests of the Canaanite
Baal narrated in the first Book of Kings.

Come down, O Christ, and help me! reach thy hand,
    For I am drowning in a stormier sea
    Than Simon on thy lake of Galilee:
The wine of life is spilt upon the sand,
My heart is as some famine-murdered land
    Whence all good things have perished utterly,
    And well I know my soul in Hell must lie
If I this night before God's throne should stand.
"He sleeps perchance, or rideth to the chase,
    Like Baal, when his prophets howled that name
    From morn to noon on Carmel's smitten height."
Nay, peace, I shall behold, before the night,
    The feet of brass, the robe more white than flame,
    The wounded hands, the weary human face.

Hélas

"Hélas ("Alas!") speaks poignantly of this aesthete's sense of the
price he has paid for the "honey of romance," his feeling of spiritual
loss, regret, and anguish over his wasted gifts and debauched life.
The reference is to Chapter 14 of the first Book of Samuel. The
first two lines of this sonnet succinctly sum up the attitude,
amounting to doctrine, that the poets of the nineties assumed
toward both life and art.

To drift with every passion till my soul
Is a stringed lute on which all winds can play,
Is it for this that I have given away
Mine ancient wisdom and austere control?
Methinks my life is a twice-written scroll
Scrawled over on some boyish holiday
With idle songs for pipe and virelay,
Which do but mar the secret of the whole.
Surely there was a time I might have trod
The sunlit heights, and from life's dissonance
Struck one clear chord to reach the ears of God.
Is that time dead? lo! with a little rod
I did but touch the honey of romance—
And must I lose a soul's inheritance?

On the Sale by Auction of Keats' Love Letters

*In his indignation on behalf of an earlier poet, Wilde here strikes
a more manly and independent note than sounds in his other sonnets.
The implication that love, beauty, and art are alien to the buying and
selling of a mercantile age is a recurring note in the verse of the
nineteenth century. Note Wilde's implicit analogy between God
and poet in the sestet, his aesthete's sense not merely of the beauty
but, more strongly, of the divinity of artistic creation.*

These are the letters which Endymion wrote
    To one he loved in secret, and apart.
    And now the brawlers of the auction mart
Bargain and bid for each poor blotted note,
Ay! for each separate pulse of passion quote
    The merchant's price. I think they love not art
    Who break the crystal of a poet's heart
That small and sickly eyes may glare and gloat.

Is it not said that many years ago,
    In a far Eastern town, some soldiers ran
    With torches through the midnight, and began
To wrangle for mean raiment, and to throw

Dice for the garments of a wretched man,
Not knowing the God's wonder, or His woe?

Ernest Dowson (1867–1900)

A Last Word

*This sonnet, which clearly reveals in much of its phraseology the
influence of Swinburne, should be compared with Christina
Rossetti's "Rest" (p. 126).*

Let us go hence: the night is now at hand;
   The day is overworn, the birds all flown;
   And we have reaped the crops the gods have sown;
Despair and death; deep darkness o'er the land,
Broods like an owl; we cannot understand
   Laughter or tears, for we have only known
   Surpassing vanity: vain things alone
Have driven our perverse and aimless band.

Let us go hence, somewhither strange and cold,
   To Hollow Lands where just men and unjust
Find end of labour, where's rest for the old,
   Freedom to all from love and fear and lust.
Twine our torn hands! O pray the earth enfold
   Our life-sick hearts and turn them into dust.

To One in Bedlam

*Note again the influence of Swinburne, in such phrases as "men
who sow and reap," imitated from Swinburne's "The Garden of
Proserpine." Dowson here uses the six-foot alexandrine line instead
of iambic pentameter. The choice of theme is characteristic of the*

period and shows the influence of such French poets as
Baudelaire, Rimbaud, and Verlaine.

> With delicate, mad hands, behind his sordid bars,
> Surely he hath his posies, which they tear and twine;
> Those scentless wisps of straw, that miserably line
> His strait, caged universe, whereat the dull world stares,
>
> Pedant and pitiful. O, how his rapt gaze wars
> With their stupidity! Know they what dreams divine
> Lift his long, laughing reveries like enchanted wine,
> And make his melancholy germane to the stars?
>
> O lamentable brother! if those pity thee,
> Am I not fain of all thy lone eyes promise me;
> Half a fool's kingdom, far from men who sow and reap,
> All their days, vanity? Better than mortal flowers,
> Thy moon-kissed roses seem: better than love or sleep,
> The star-crowned solitude of thine oblivious hours!

Lionel Johnson (*1867–1902*)

The Age of a Dream

Again the alexandrine line, slowing the movement and lending a
more meditative tone that suits the subject. Observe that Johnson's
nostalgia for the past, even for its religion, is wholly on aesthetic
grounds. It is "the death of beauty and the death of grace"
he mourns, not the death of faith.

> Imageries of dreams reveal a gracious age:
> Black armour, falling lace, and altar lights at morn.
> The courtesy of Saints, their gentleness and scorn,
> Lights on an earth more fair, than shone from Plato's page:
> The courtesy of knights, fair calm and sacred rage:

The courtesy of love, sorrow for love's sake borne.
Vanished, those high conceits! Desolate and forlorn,
We hunger against hope for that lost heritage.

Gone now, the carven work! Ruined, the golden shrine!
No more the glorious organs pour their voice divine;
No more rich frankincense drifts through the Holy Place:
Now from the broken tower, what solemn bell still tolls,
Mourning what piteous death? Answer, O saddened souls!
Who mourn the death of beauty and the death of grace.

Lord Alfred Douglas (1870–1945)

Impression de Nuit—London

An imitation, in manner and matter, of the French symbolists.
Note particularly the symbolist imagery of the sestet.

See what a mass of gems the city wears
Upon her broad live bosom! row on row
Rubies and emeralds and amethysts glow.
See that huge circle like a necklace, stares
With thousands of bold eyes to heaven, and dares
The golden stars to dim the lamps below,
And in the mirror of the mire I know
The moon has left her image unawares.

That's the great town at night: I see her breasts,
Pricked out with lamps they stand like huge black towers,
I think they move! I hear her panting breath.
And that's her head where the tiara rests.
And in her brain, through lanes as dark as death,
Men creep like thoughts . . . the lamps are like pale flowers.

The Twentieth Century

A century ago Hopkins "broke the new wood" in the extraordinary sonnets we are still learning how to value. There have been no experiments so radical since. The sonnets of the twentieth century exhibit the persistence of tradition to as great a degree as they do the impulse of change. In our day the argument over "correct" sonnet structure has been silenced and contemporary poets use or discard the conventions as they wish. Thus, a collection of sonnets written in this century exhibits all manner of variety. Rhyme, meter, and syntax alike are handled with a license unknown until Hopkins. Yet the strict Shakespearean and Italian sonnet still exists alongside the experimental, and even the freest of modern sonnets look almost conventional by comparison with "The Windhover" or "Hurrahing in Harvest."

Throughout its long history, the most striking characteristic of the sonnet has been its protean ability to adapt to new subjects, new viewpoints, new worlds of thought and feeling, new words and ways of using language. It still speaks of the old themes of love, of nature, and of death, for the world and the self are the necessary material and condition of art as they are of life. But it speaks in words and images drawn from the contemporary scene and the disciplines of contemporary thought. Its subject matter has broadened to include new worlds without and within: war and social crisis and the innermost privacies of emotion and perception. It speaks above all in a new tone and stands in a new relation to the reader.

It is, more than any other characteristic, the voice that speaks that distinguishes the twentieth-century sonnet. Lover or satirist, soldier or scholar, recluse or man of affairs, the contemporary poet is a private person reporting or reflecting upon felt experience to another private person. Gone are the abstractions, the huge, cloudy generalities loved by the Victorians. Gone with them is the solemnity, the reverence, the self-importance, the stilted manner, the pompousness that lurks in the wings of the nineteenth century. What has changed is man's conception of himself and his world and, therefore, the poet's attitude toward the reader and his aim in writing the poem.

He no longer wishes to *present* but to *involve,* to engage the reader immediately and forcefully with the experience explored in the poem. There is thus no distance between poet and reader, between reader and poem. The contemporary poet employs all his technical skill and all his imaginative, moral, and emotional force to draw the reader in, to engage him—often with violence—not with a static *object* but with a *process.*

The modern sonnet, then, is above all else immediate, personal, and concrete. Its language is simple, colloquial, often slangy; its manner informal; its syntax unhampered by rules; its rhythms and movement individual, springing from subject and mood rather than conforming to any conventional pattern. It employs irregular stresses, lines of variable length, casual and arbitrary rhyme schemes, and half rhymes often in place of true ones. Whatever its subject or its particular technical devices, its characteristic concern is with direct, intimate experience whether sensuous, emotional, or spiritual.

In our century the sonnet has continued but extended and redefined the Victorian vision of man alone in an alien universe. It goes beyond any of the Victorian sonnets in its sense of the existential nature of life, the death of God, the inexorable flow of time, and especially the unfathomed and treacherous depths within the self. The Victorians perceived the dissolution of old certainties and the coming of social crisis. The modern poet lives in the very presence of crisis, amid war, revolution, and social change. Where the Victorians took refuge in some form of withdrawal, the poet of our day knows that there is no hiding place—neither in faith, nor in tradition, nor in nature, nor in art, nor even in love itself. He believes in nothing save the reality and the value of his own experience. Accepting only what he can "prove upon his pulses," as Keats long ago declared, the twentieth-century sonneteer loves the beauty of nature without faith or hope and celebrates the sweetness of love without expectation of permanence here or hereafter. He eyes past illusions of progress and perfectibility with ironic mockery. No longer reinforced by common values and universal truths, he lives—or tries to live—in the passing moment he alone possesses surely and laments that his nature will not allow him to abandon reason with its abstractions and ideals and immerse himself in the flux of experience. "Acquainted with the night," in Frost's phrase, the contemporary poet has eaten the fruit of the tree of the knowledge of good and evil and faced the possibility that evil may be the end of all experience and of all desire.

Such a description suggests that gloom and doom are the dominant notes of the twentieth-century sonnet. Oddly enough, this is not so. Most modern sonnets, however dark in outlook, are high-spirited, full of zest even for tragedy. Love poems are tender and romantic or sensuous and passionate. They neither idealize, sentimentalize, nor falsify; they celebrate, declaring that love is good even among the ruins. And the delight of the metaphysical poets in wit and word play has returned, along with their synthesis of thought with feeling and with passion. Playfulness and mockery sparkle amid the darkness, and a sonnet on a funeral begins with a wry pun. Many sonnets are intensely dramatic in manner, using scene and dialogue to objectify and make more vivid the experience they record. Modern sonnets may, indeed, be gloomy, but they are never dreary as so many Victorian sonnets are. If they announce doom, they do so, despite Eliot, not with a whimper but in ringing tones and frequently with laughter. They have more stomach for disaster than the Victorians had for benefits and blessings.

Of traditional sonneteers in our century, whether British or American, none has written finer sonnets than those of Edwin Arlington Robinson. Completely conventional in form, his sonnets recall those of Shakespeare in themes and in tone, and the best are not inferior to Shakespeare's. Almost alone among the moderns Robinson successfully assumes the old, grand manner, the superb arrogance of the artist self-dedicated to the service of the god. "Many Are Called" and "Verlaine" assert with the old intonation the old faith in the supreme value of art. "The Sheaves" is a magical re-creation of a characteristic Renaissance theme, the passing beauty of the world. In such poems as this Robinson seems like a throwback, though in somewhat more modern diction, to the early days of the English sonnet. But Robinson too has other sides and a wider range, and such poems as "Aaron Stark" and "New England" show his more modern qualities of psychological penetration and dry, tongue-in-cheek humor.

George Santayana, John Masefield, Hilaire Belloc, and Charlotte Mew belong in most respects to the nineteenth rather than to the twentieth century. They are traditionalists in form and in theme, in diction and in manner. There is no real difference between the sonnets of Masefield and those of Robert Bridges, his senior by a generation. Both are Platonists, celebrating that beauty which, known in the flesh, exists in "the universal mind." Belloc and Mew strike the note of weariness and longing for repose heard so often in the preceding century, and the smooth, fluid movement and sound of their verse is an old felicity that soothes and satisfies rather than stimulates. Santayana too is old-fashioned in manner and language, his sense of isolation and his invocation of traditional faith also Victorian in feeling and in effect.

Conrad Aiken, Edna St. Vincent Millay, Winifred Welles, Leonie Adams, and Archibald MacLeish exhibit a more modern handling of old conventions and the beginning of new viewpoints and new emphases. Aiken's celebration of nature, of love, and of art preserves the mold of the Shakespearean sonnet and the Shakespearean emphasis on the power of love and art to dominate the flux of nature. But his vision is a more existential one, a vision of man's need and man's power to create his own meaning and value in a world where the one certainty is flow and change. Adams, Welles, and MacLeish all, though in very different ways, use the traditional form for a modern vision of man's fate: not only forever alone but forever burdened with the consciousness of his aloneness even while sharing a common doom. Millay's materials are the familiar ones, the ecstasy and agony of love, the power of art, the sureness of death. In many ways, she too is a traditionalist. Yet more important than the use of tradition by these writers is their departure from it, though their poems only hint at changes that, in other hands, have more impact. These are changes in diction, in image, in movement, and in that all-important quality given by the poet's relation to subject and reader.

The effect of "Cruciform" resides not merely in the simplicity of its language combined with the poignancy of its theme, but even more in the direct and sad simplicity with which the poet addresses us. It is a simplicity as clear and unmannered as that of Christina Rossetti, but Christina does not talk to us. She talks to herself, to her beloved, to God: we merely overhear what she says. In "Thought's End," though the poet seems to be speaking to herself, she is not; she is reporting to us an experience we share with her. Aiken sees the eternal flux not only in the winds of space and the alternations of day and night, but in the bloodstream, in the hand that shapes and holds the moment; there is no distance between him and his perceptions, between him and his beloved, between him and us. MacLeish presents his apocalyptic vision in powerfully concrete, mundane, individual, personal images drawn from an experience familiar to us all. Millay mocks the romantic emotion she feels by adopting a deliberately antiromantic posture, flippant and cynical; by refusing either to deceive or to be deceived by lover or by love. Shakespeare and Sidney would recognize the mockery. But it is not so much the mockery itself as the voice with which it speaks that is modern.

Robert Frost, only five years younger than Robinson, speaks in the new voice. Though they are freer than Robinson's in their use of structural conventions, his sonnets vary and depart from the traditional forms in relatively minor ways. Like so many earlier poets he is an observer and a lover of nature; so much so that during his long life he was oversold as the poet of a homely New England pastoralism. But Frost is distinctively modern in viewpoint and even more in tone and manner.

"Design" is darker by far in its implications than Hopkins' so-called "terrible" sonnets. Here the "argument from design," traditional proof of the existence of God, is invoked to question both His existence and His nature if He does exist. Hardy, darkest of the Victorians, had suggested that God, if indeed He did exist, might be a kind of cosmic imbecile "dying downward," but had confessed in softer mood to being a meliorist, one who hoped that improvement might be looked for. Frost who, toward the end of his life, seems to have come close to Christian orthodoxy, nevertheless has a vision now and then of evil without and within more radical than that of Hardy. Frost's tone, so personal, so conversational, so apparently unmoved by any of the anguish felt by Hopkins or by Hardy, brings us closer to what he sees and feels. He paints in the octave a picture, a scene, in which everything is done by suggestion rather than statement. The questions of the sestet are quiet and even until, abruptly, shockingly, the final question explodes on our awareness, to be followed at once by the final, understated, almost throwaway line concealing the last and most lethal punch. It is the variation and manipulation of tone even more than diction and image that produces the sonnet's tremendous impact. In "Once By The Pacific" we observe with the poet the personification of cosmic doom, the living menace of the universe itself rising with rage and "dark intent" and—more terrifying still—God's quiet voice, the umpire ending the game. It is not a grand so much as a very person-to-person apocalypse that we are being made to feel. "Acquainted with the Night" in an even more personal and intimate way evokes the evil of man himself, man in society. Always, whatever Frost sees or feels, his voice is that of a particular individual taking a friend into his confidence. Frost's voice is peculiarly his own, for it combines with other qualities, especially with his deliberate adoption of a pose as shrewd but unsophisticated philosopher, to produce the particular flavor of his verse. But in the intimacy he establishes with the reader, the lack of formality and of distance, his voice is that of the twentieth century itself.

What is true of Frost is much more obviously true of E. E. Cummings. At first sight Cummings' sonnets look as if they fractured all tradition. And so they do—in some ways. Even more than did Hopkins, Cummings dispenses with traditional syntax, wrenches word order, uses condensations and ellipses, coins words and uses ordinary words in extraordinary and often outrageous ways, employs slang and profanity, and generally plays with language like a fiendishly skillful verbal juggler. His trademark is his refusal to employ normal capitalization and punctuation, and even poems that reveal themselves clearly when read aloud look strange and sometimes unintelligible on the printed page.

Cummings' techniques are, and are meant to be, deceptive. Traditional in some ways, as in his more romantic love poetry, he is a true modern in his desire above everything to engage the reader immediately and violently with the experience of the poem. Poetry is not for him a stately dance of words but a wrestling match. He dispenses with traditional structures and traditional punctuation because he feels they interpose a barrier between the reader and the poem. His verse, when it succeeds, compels an almost physical involvement. It lays hold on us and forces us to feel the strength and the meaning it embodies.

Since Cummings' faith is in sensory and emotional experience, it is natural that his verse should celebrate erotic love and repudiate those aspects of contemporary society that deny and detract from the fullness and richness of life. His love poetry is both romantic and sensual, more sensual than that of Rossetti, and more romantic than that of any other sonneteer, ancient or modern. And his satire on a mechanical and artificial society and on the banality, hypocrisy, and humbug it engenders is both playful and savage. Since Cummings the sonnet has frequently been used for purposes of social satire, but never more successfully.

The twentieth century was born not in the calendar year 1900 but amid the convulsions of World War I and during the period of disillusion and social upheaval that followed in the twenties. It is no wonder that the sonnet should in our century have become a vehicle for satire. And since war of some sort has been the constant condition of the world since 1913, it is no wonder that many good modern sonnets are war poems.

Rupert Brooke, most gifted of the Georgian poets, died in 1915, before he could experience the reality of modern warfare. His sonnet "The Soldier" was intensely moving to his own generation and can still move us if we are able to achieve sufficient detachment from the historical and social realities of our century. Brooke, whose verse is so often spoiled by his self-conscious poses, here for once has his mind on his subject rather than on himself. He achieves a true expression of a real, though perhaps old-fashioned patriotism, in which love speaks without bravado. But this is the last time that a poet can speak like this of death in war. In Brooke's own day, other young men who had seen more than did he were already speaking with a different accent. Edmund Blunden employs Keatsian diction and imagery for a bitterly ironic denunciation of a tradition that had led only to "death and lice." Wilfred Owen, greatest of World War I poets, in one of the finest sonnets of the century, "Anthem for Doomed Youth," gravely mocks the Christian rites of peacetime death now parodied by guns and shells, suggesting the futility and negation of all traditional attitudes and values in face of the monstrous reality of war.

Owen was killed a week before the Armistice, and the poems he had scribbled on scrap paper in the trenches and in the hospital were unpublished and unknown. They were edited and published early in the twenties by his friend Siegfried Sassoon and by Edith Sitwell, both poets themselves. These poems strongly influenced a new generation of young poets in England, partly through their technical virtuosity and partly because Owen had categorically rejected the doctrine of art for art's sake and had devoted his mature poetry to depicting with unflinching honesty the physical, social, and spiritual horrors of modern war. Owen had experimented with great success with a technique of half-rhymes, in which the consonant sound remains while the vowel changes—*killed/cold, fooling/filling*—and had employed a symphonic variety of sound effects. Succeeding poets have learned the lessons he taught, along with those of Hopkins. W. H. Auden, Stephen Spender, Rex Warner, George Barker, Dylan Thomas, Christopher Hassall, among poets represented in this volume, all show Owen's influence; and younger poets take all such matters as half-rhyme, irregular stress, variable line length, and individual rhyme schemes for granted. The sonnet has adjusted as naturally to the introduction of these new techniques as it has to new themes alien to the old tradition: war, social crisis, satire, "the journey within."

Yet, at present, our leading poets—with few exceptions—seem not to be writing sonnets of any sort. American poets especially tend to reject formal patterns, leaving each poem to find its own appropriate and organic form. Say *sonnet* today to anyone except a captive audience of students and the usual response is a tolerant smile. Is the sonnet in the 1970's a fossil, incapable of containing or expressing the meaning of experience in the modern world? Like Eliot's "Hollow Men," is it "shape without form, shade without colour/Paralysed force, gesture without motion"?

At least one contemporary poet, Margaret Avison, has written a "Sonnet Against Sonnets," ostensibly announcing the death and—worse still—the mummification of this ancient form.

Butterfly Bones; or Sonnet Against Sonnets

The cyanide jar seals life, as sonnets move
towards final stiffness. Cased in a white glare
these specimens stare for peering boys, to prove
strange certainties. Plane dogsled and safari
assure continuing range. The sweep-net skill,
the patience, learning, leave all living stranger.
Insect—or poem—waits for the fix, the frill
precision can effect, brilliant with danger.
What law and wonder the museum spectres
bespeak is cryptic for the shivery wings,
the world cut-diamond-eyed, those eyes' reflectors,

or herbal grass, sunned motes, fierce listening.
Might sheened and rigid trophies strike men blind
like Adam's lexicon locked in the mind?

The form is wholly traditional, that of the strict Shakespearean sonnet, and the enjambement of the first few lines, though more emphatic than usual, is certainly no innovation. On the surface, this traditional form is being employed to mock tradition: sonnets, the poet tells us, like museum specimens, preserve a form from which all life has departed. But poets, as Plato knew, are notorious liars. What is the poem itself telling us?

The sonnet, paradoxically, is giving the lie to all its creator seems to be saying. The very rigidity of its form, combined with a wholly contemporary diction, imagery, and syntax, is what makes it effective. Its theme is presented by means of dramatic contrasts—death/life, abstract/concrete, formula/experience, knowing/being—made vivid in figures that glance off and mirror one another until the poem becomes a prism reflecting from various angles the point it makes. The *cyanide jar* judges the *Plane dogsled and safari* and *The sweep-net skill* that lead to it; the *final stiffness, museum spectres,* and *sheened and rigid trophies* contrast with the *shivery wings* of life; the *white glare, brilliant with danger* with the *world cut-diamond-eyed, those eyes' reflectors;* the *stare* of the specimens—a blind stare—becomes blindness itself that strikes living men in the penultimate line; the *peering* boys, knowing death only through sight, contrasts both with the *world cut-diamond-eyed* and with *herbal grass, sunned motes, fierce listening,* all the sensory experience of living creatures; *locked in the mind* swings round to the sealed cyanide jar of the first line, reminding us that to be locked in the mind alone is death.

In its use of traditional form to express a peculiarly modern point of view in modern language and in images drawn from the contemporary world, in the brilliant and ironic paradox whereby what it *is* denies what it *says,* the poem is a fine example of the contemporary sonnet and visible proof that that form is as viable now as it has been for more than four hundred years. Wyatt would still —though occasionally with difficulty—recognize its form and many twentieth century sonneteers are still speaking out of tradition. But there is ample proof also that new wine can still be poured from the old bottles and that old conventions can be used by new poets in new ways.

George Santayana (1863–1952)

"O world, thou choosest not the better part"

O world, thou choosest not the better part!
It is not wisdom to be only wise,
And on the inward vision close the eyes,
But it is wisdom to believe the heart.
Columbus found a world, and had no chart,
Save one that faith deciphered in the skies;
To trust the soul's invincible surmise
Was all his science and his only art.
Our knowledge is a torch of smoky pine
That lights the pathway but one step ahead
Across a void of mystery and dread.
Bid, then, the tender light of faith to shine
By which alone the mortal heart is led
Unto the thinking of the thought divine.

"I would I might forget . . ."

I would I might forget that I am I,
And break the heavy chain that binds me fast,
Whose links about myself my deeds have cast.
What in the body's tomb doth buried lie
Is boundless; 'tis the spirit of the sky,
Lord of the future, guardian of the past,
And soon must forth, to know his own at last.
In his large life to live, I fain would die.
Happy the dumb beast, hungering for food,

But calling not his suffering his own;
Blessèd the angel, gazing on all good,
But knowing not he sits upon a throne;
Wretched the mortal, pondering his mood,
And doomed to know his aching heart alone.

"Deem not, because you see me in the press"

Deem not, because you see me in the press
Of this world's children run my fated race,
That I blaspheme against a proffered grace,
Or leave unlearned the love of holiness.
I honour not that sanctity the less
Whose aureole illumines not my face,
But dare not tread the secret, holy place
To which the priest and prophet have access.
For some are born to be beatified
By anguish, and by grievous penance done;
And some, to furnish forth the age's pride,
And to be praised of men beneath the sun;
And some are born to stand perplexed aside
From so much sorrow—of whom I am one.

William Butler Yeats (1865–1939)

Leda and the Swan

Magnificent, compressed sensuality. A poem that begins in violence, describes the rape of Leda by Zeus in the shape of a swan, and ends by questioning the result of such a union. The poem is a paradox—Leda is unwilling, but unable to deny "the feathered glory"; she is "terrified," but "caught up"; she is "mastered"; the swan is "indifferent." Indeed, can humanity and divinity be fused? Can intellect and emotion combine?

A sudden blow: the great wings beating still
Above the staggering girl, her thighs caressed
By the dark webs, her nape caught in his bill,
He holds her helpless breast upon his breast.

How can those terrified vague fingers push
The feathered glory from her loosening thighs?
And how can body, laid in that white rush,
But feel the strange heart beating where it lies?

A shudder in the loins engenders there
The broken wall, the burning roof and tower
And Agamemnon dead.
                              Being so caught up,
So mastered by the brute blood of the air,
Did she put on his knowledge with his power
Before the indifferent beak could let her drop?

Charlotte Mew (1869–1928)

Not for That City

Not for that city of the level sun,
        Its golden streets and glittering gates ablaze—
        The shadeless, sleepless city of white days,
White nights, or nights and days that are as one—
We weary, when all is said, all thought, all done.
        We strain our eyes beyond this dusk to see
        What, from the threshold of eternity,
We shall step into. No, I think we shun
The splendor of that everlasting glare,
        The clamor of that never-ending song.
        And if for anything we greatly long,
It is for some remote and quiet stair

Which winds to silence and a space of sleep
Too sound for waking and for dreams too deep.

Edwin Arlington Robinson (*1869–1935*)

New England

This sonnet should be compared with Lowell's "Concord," (p. 217).
Lowell's subject is the same, and his form as conventional; all else
is different: diction, imagery, movement, tone, wit, perspective,
and attitude. These two poems alone demonstrate how flexibly
the traditional sonnet form accommodates itself to different purposes
and different styles.

Here where the wind is always north-north-east
And children learn to walk on frozen toes,
Wonder begets an envy of all those
Who boil elsewhere with such a lyric yeast

Of love that you will hear them at a feast
Where demons would appeal for some repose,
Still clamoring where the chalice overflows
And crying wildest who have drunk the least.

Passion is here a soilure of the wits,
We're told, and Love a cross for them to bear;
Joy shivers in the corner where she knits
And Conscience always has the rocking-chair,
Cheerful as when she tortured into fits
The first cat that was ever killed by Care.

Aaron Stark

One of Robinson's psychological portraits in miniature. The poem makes an effect strikingly different from that of his sonnets in the grand manner, like "Many Are Called." Note the image, both realistic and dramatically appropriate, of the fourth line.

Withal a meagre man was Aaron Stark,
Cursed and unkempt, shrewd, shrivelled, and morose.
A miser was he, with a miser's nose,
And eyes like little dollars in the dark.
His thin, pinched mouth was nothing but a mark;
And when he spoke there came like sullen blows
Through scattered fangs a few snarled words and close,
As if a cur were chary of its bark.

Glad for the murmur of his hard renown,
Year after year he shambled through the town,
A loveless exile moving with a staff;
And oftentimes there crept into his ears
A sound of alien pity, touched with tears,—
And then (and only then) did Aaron laugh.

Calvary

Compare this sonnet with Wilde's "On Hearing the 'Dies Irae' Sung in the Sistine Chapel" (p. 154) and "E Tenebris" (p. 155) and note the difference in the relation of the two poets to their subject. Wilde's emotion is personal anguish and longing; Robinson's emotion, not less in intensity, is impersonal pity and indignation.

Friendless and faint, with martyred steps and slow,
Faint for the flesh, but for the spirit free,
Stung by the mob that came to see the show,
The Master toiled along to Calvary;

We gibed him, as he went, with houndish glee,
Till his dimmed eyes for us did overflow;
We cursed his vengeless hands thrice wretchedly,—
And this was nineteen hundred years ago.

But after nineteen hundred years the shame
Still clings, and we have not made good the loss
That outraged faith has entered in his name.
Ah, when shall come love's courage to be strong!
Tell me, O Lord—tell me, O Lord, how long
Are we to keep Christ writhing on the cross!

Sonnet

*Robinson combines satire here with his characteristic lofty view
of art, to comment on the sonnet scene in the nineties.*

Oh for a poet—for a beacon bright
To rift this changless glimmer of dead gray;
To spirit back the Muses, long astray,
And flush Parnassus with a newer light;
To put these little sonnet-men to flight
Who fashion, in a shrewd mechanic way,
Songs without souls, that flicker for a day,
To vanish in irrevocable night.

What does it mean, this barren age of ours?
Here are the men, the women, and the flowers,
The seasons, and the sunset, as before.
What does it mean? Shall there not one arise
To wrench one banner from the western skies,
And mark it with his name forevermore?

Verlaine

*An effective and typical mixture of realism and grandeur. The
repulsive imagery of the octave, by contrast with the sestet,*

*powerfully objectifies and dramatizes the opposition of life and art,
mortality and immortality, human sin and the beauty sinful men
can create.*

Why do you dig like long-clawed scavengers
To touch the covered corpse of him that fled
The uplands for the fens, and rioted
Like a sick satyr with doom's worshippers?
Come! let the grass grow there; and leave his verse
To tell the story of the life he led.
Let the man go: let the dead flesh be dead,
And let the worms be its biographers.

Song sloughs away the sin to find redress
In art's complete remembrance: nothing clings
For long but laurel to the stricken brow
That felt the Muse's finger; nothing less
Than hell's fulfilment of the end of things
Can blot the star that shines on Paris now.

Many Are Called

The Lord Apollo, who has never died,
Still holds alone his immemorial reign,
Supreme in an impregnable domain
That with his magic he has fortified;
And though melodious multitudes have tried
In ecstasy, in anguish, and in vain,
With invocation sacred and profane
To lure him, even the loudest are outside.

Only at unconjectured intervals,
By will of him on whom no man may gaze,
By word of him whose law no man has read,
A questing light may rift the sullen walls,
To cling where mostly its infrequent rays
Fall golden on the patience of the dead.

The Clerks

I did not think that I should find them there
When I came back again; but there they stood,
As in the days they dreamed of when young blood
Was in their cheeks and women called them fair.
Be sure, they met me with an ancient air,—
And yes, there was a shop-worn brotherhood
About them; but the men were just as good,
And just as human as they ever were.

And you that ache so much to be sublime,
And you that feed yourselves with your descent,
What comes of all your visions and your fears?
Poets and kings are but the clerks of Time,
Tiering the same dull webs of discontent,
Clipping the same sad alnage of the years.

The Sheaves

Where long the shadows of the wind had rolled,
Green wheat was yielding to the change assigned;
And as by some vast magic undivined
The world was turning slowly into gold.
Like nothing that was ever bought or sold
It waited there, the body and the mind;
And with a mighty meaning of a kind
That tells the more the more it is not told.

So in a land where all days are not fair,
Fair days went on till on another day
A thousand golden sheaves were lying there,
Shining and still, but not for long to stay—
As if a thousand girls with golden hair
Might rise from where they slept and go away.

Hilaire Belloc (1870–1953)

"We will not whisper . . ."

We will not whisper, we have found the place
Of silence and the endless halls of sleep.
And that which breathes alone throughout the deep
The end and the beginning: and the face
Between the level brows of whose blind eyes
Lie plenary contentment, full surcease
Of violence, and the passionless long peace
Wherein we lose our human lullabies.

Look up and tell the immeasurable height
Between the vault of the world and your dear head;
That's death, my little sister, and the night
Which was our Mother beckons us to bed,
   Where large oblivion in her house is laid
   For us tired children, now our games are played.

Robert Frost (1875–1963)

Design

*Diction and imagery combine, particularly in the octave, to suggest
the hideous unnaturalness—from the human point of view—
of this design for death. The* dimpled spider, fat and white *sounds
like a repulsive baby; the moth resembles a* white piece of rigid
satin cloth, *all three adjectives suggesting death in different ways;*
mixed ready to begin the morning right *is as apparently cheerfully*

*commonplace as a TV coffee commercial, except for the sinister
context and the pun on* right *("rite"), immediately reinforced and
driven home in the next line;* froth *suggests corruption, illness, or
madness;* dead wings *repeats the theme of unnaturalness and*
paper kite *harks back to the deathlike rigidity of the satin cloth.
In the sestet* steered *is particularly effective in conjunction with the
poet's rhetorical questions, culminating in the appalling insight
of the last two lines.*

> I found a dimpled spider, fat and white,
> On a white heal-all, holding up a moth
> Like a white piece of rigid satin cloth—
> Assorted characters of death and blight
> Mixed ready to begin the morning right,
> Like the ingredients of a witches' broth—
> A snow-drop spider, a flower like a froth,
> And dead wings carried like a paper kite.
>
> What had that flower to do with being white,
> The wayside blue and innocent heal-all?
> What brought the kindred spider to that height,
> Then steered the white moth thither in the night?
> What but design of darkness to appall?—
> If design govern in a thing so small.

Acquainted with the Night

Frost here adapts terza rima, *the rhyme scheme of Dante's*
The Divine Comedy, *to sonnet use. The poem vividly suggests
the loneliness and menace of modern urban life.*

> I have been one acquainted with the night.
> I have walked out in rain—and back in rain.
> I have outwalked the furthest city light.
>
> I have looked down the saddest city lane.
> I have passed by the watchman on his beat
> And dropped my eyes, unwilling to explain.

I have stood still and stopped the sound of feet
When far away an interrupted cry
Came over houses from another street,

But not to call me back or say good-by;
And further still at an unearthly height,
One luminary clock against the sky

Proclaimed the time was neither wrong nor right.
I have been one acquainted with the night.

Putting in the Seed

*Through scene, image, and tone the poet creates a sense of the unity
of man and nature. The relationship of husband and wife is linked
to the* springtime passion *that plants the seed and watches its birth
from the earth that nourishes all life. The birth of the seedling
is rendered in terms suggesting human birth;* the earth crumbs
remind us that *supper's on the table; all is done delicately,
indirectly, by suggestion.*

You come to fetch me from my work tonight
When supper's on the table, and we'll see
If I can leave off burying the white
Soft petals fallen from the apple tree
(Soft petals, yes, but not so barren quite,
Mingled with these, smooth bean and wrinkled pea;)
And go along with you ere you lose sight
Of what you came for and become like me,
Slave to a springtime passion for the earth.
How Love burns through the Putting in the Seed
On through the watching for that early birth
When, just as the soil tarnishes with weed,
The sturdy seedling with arched body comes
Shouldering its way and shedding the earth crumbs.

The Silken Tent

A poem of compliment, which should be compared with Cowper's "To Mrs. Unwin" (p. 64), and Milton's "On the Religious Memory of Mrs. Catharine Thomson" (p. 59). The affinities of this poem, however, are rather with the seventeenth-century lyric, especially with Robert Herrick. Frost's diction and syntax are as supple and pliant as the central image on which the comparison turns, and the effortless grace of the sonnet's movement is as effective as the analogy in describing its subject.

> She is as in a field a silken tent
> At midday when a sunny summer breeze
> Has dried the dew and all its ropes relent,
> So that in guys it gently sways at ease,
> And its supporting central cedar pole,
> That is its pinnacle to heavenward
> And signifies the sureness of the soul,
> Seems to owe naught to any single cord,
> But strictly held by none, is loosely bound
> By countless silken ties of love and thought
> To everything on earth the compass round,
> And only by one's going slightly taut
> In the capriciousness of summer air
> Is of the slightest bondage made aware.

Once by the Pacific

Compare with Campbell's "Familiar Daemon" (p. 205) for its different use of rhyming couplets. These cannot be considered an innovation: see, for instance, Shakespeare's Sonnet 126.

> The shattered water made a misty din.
> Great waves looked over others coming in,
> And thought of doing something to the shore
> That water never did to land before.

The clouds were low and hairy in the skies,
Like locks blown forward in the gleam of eyes.
You could not tell, and yet it looked as if
The shore was lucky in being backed by cliff,
The cliff in being backed by continent;
It looked as if a night of dark intent
Was coming, and not only a night, an age.
Someone had better be prepared for rage.
There would be more than ocean-water broken
Before God's last *Put out the Light* was spoken.

The Oven Bird

A good example of Frost's ability to use realistic natural scene and image to suggest larger and more abstract meanings. That other fall we name the fall *is both the autumn of the year and, by implication, the plight of man in a fallen world.*

There is a singer everyone has heard,
Loud, a mid-summer and a mid-wood bird,
Who makes the solid tree trunks sound again.
He says that leaves are old and that for flowers
Mid-summer is to spring as one to ten.
He says the early petal-fall is past
When pear and cherry bloom went down in showers
On sunny days a moment overcast;
And comes that other fall we name the fall.
He says the highway dust is over all.
The bird would cease and be as other birds
But that he knows in singing not to sing.
The question that he frames in all but words
Is what to make of a diminished thing.

John Masefield (1878–1967)

"Here in the self . . ."

Here in the self is all that man can know
Of Beauty, all the wonder, all the power,
All the unearthly color, all the glow,
Here in the self which withers like a flower;
Here in the self which fades as hours pass,
And droops and dies and rots and is forgotten,
Sooner, by ages, than the mirroring glass
In which it sees its glory still unrotten.
Here in the flesh, within the flesh, behind,
Swift in the blood and throbbing on the bone,
Beauty herself, the universal mind,
Eternal April wandering alone,
The god, the holy ghost, the atoning lord,
Here in the flesh, the never yet explored.

"Flesh, I have knocked . . ."

Flesh, I have knocked at many a dusty door,
Gone down full many a windy midnight lane,
Probed in old walls and felt along the floor,
Pressed in blind hope the lighted window-pane.
But useless all, though sometimes, when the moon
Was full in heaven and the sea was full,
Along my body's alleys came a tune
Played in the tavern by the Beautiful.
Then for an instant I have felt at point
To find and seize her, whosoe'er she be,
Whether some saint whose glory does anoint
Those whom she loves, or but a part of me,

Or something that the things not understood
Make for their uses out of flesh and blood.

Donald C. Babcock (1885–   )

America

*A traditional Shakespearean sonnet. The poet, with the voice of a
contemporary American, speaks of his country with bitterness,
describing it as "no new device at all." America's disdain for other
countries who failed to win the fight for liberty, becomes the poet's
disdain for America. Confidence turns to cynicism: the lessons of
history, the inability of liberty to survive, "bide" in the sestet as a
reminder of America's emptiness and her failure to learn from "all
things old." So the sonnet moves from America described as "first
fruits of the West" in line 2 to "A famine of the heart" in line 14.*

So, then, we were no new device at all,
We who were born the first fruits of the West.
Or so we fancied. Oh, we stood so tall,
We looked abroad and smiled at all the rest:—
They dwelt in Europe's tombs, they dwelt in shadow;
Their forests fell in dust; mold and the blight
Lay on the vine; the moss crept on the meadow;
The doom had come on peasant, priest, and knight.
And over us, who would not stop to glean
Among the echoes of their precious word,
Nor doubted that our liberty must mean
The advent of an ultimate accord,
Bide now as ignorance of all things old,
A famine of the heart, and bitter cold.

Ezra Pound (*1885–*)

A Virginal

This sonnet shows Pound's knowledge of convention and his skill in adapting it. It is romantic in theme, attitude, and atmosphere; and the pastoral imagery, old-fashioned word usage, and light feminine rhymes work together to produce an exquisitely delicate effect.

No, no! Go from me. I have left her lately.
I will not spoil my sheath with lesser brightness,
For my surrounding air hath a new lightness;
Slight are her arms, yet they have bound me straitly
And left me cloaked as with a gauze of æther;
As with sweet leaves; as with subtle clearness.
Oh, I have picked up magic in her nearness
To sheathe me half in half the things that sheathe her.
No, no! Go from me. I have still the flavour,
Soft as spring wind that's come from birchen bowers.
Green come the shoots, aye April in the branches,
As winter's wound with her sleight hand she staunches,
Hath of the trees a likeness of the savour:
As white their bark, so white this lady's hours.

Rupert Brooke (*1887–1915*)

The Soldier

If I should die, think only this of me:
    That there's some corner of a foreign field

That is for ever England. There shall be
　In that rich earth a richer dust concealed;
A dust whom England bore, shaped, made aware,
　Gave, once, her flowers to love, her ways to roam,
A body of England's, breathing English air,
　Washed by the rivers, blest by suns of home.

And think, this heart, all evil shed away,
　A pulse in the eternal mind, no less
　　Gives somewhere back the thoughts by England given;
Her sights and sounds; dreams happy as her day;
　And laughter, learnt of friends; and gentleness,
　　In hearts at peace, under an English heaven.

A Channel Passage

This sonnet is of more historical interest than intrinsic merit.
Subject, diction, and manner alike were startling and disagreeable
to readers at the time, and Brooke's publisher, Edward Marsh,
thought himself daring to publish such verse. Though the poem
exhibits the somewhat adolescent cleverness that marks so much of
Brooke's work, it also shows a young poet's honest reaction
against the worn out clichés and conventions of the romantic
tradition. The sonnet has travelled a long way since Petrarch,
though perhaps not so far as Brooke thought.

The damned ship lurched and slithered. Quiet and quick
　My cold gorge rose; the long sea rolled; I knew
I must think hard of something, or be sick;
　And could think hard of only one thing—*you!*
You, you alone could hold my fancy ever!
　And with you memories come, sharp pain, and dole.
Now there's a choice—heartache or tortured liver!
　A sea-sick body, or a you-sick soul!

Do I forget you? Retchings twist and tie me,
　Old meat, good meals, brown gobbets, up I throw.
Do I remember? Acrid return and slimy,

The sobs and slobber of a last years woe.
And still the sick ship rolls. 'Tis hard, I tell ye,
To choose 'twixt love and nausea, heart and belly.

Robinson Jeffers (1887–1962)

The Cruel Falcon

A fine example of how essential sonnet qualities—balance, contrast, parallelism, precision of image, conciseness of thought, a large theme successfully treated in small compass—may be preserved in a very free treatment of conventional form. Note the balanced opposition of the two quatrains of the octave, in which the lives of contemplation and of action are sharply defined in vivid and shocking images; the break between octave and sestet; the way in which the expository and descriptive sestet contrasts with, yet comments upon, the thought of the octave. Jeffers' nihilism, the nausea at human life he so often expresses, his embrace of death and reversal of traditional human values, here find expression both briefer and far more powerful than in most of his longer poems.

Contemplation would make a good life, keep it strict, only
The eyes of a desert skull drinking the sun,
Too intense for flesh, lonely
Exultations of white bone;
Pure action would make a good life, let it be sharp-
Set between the throat and the knife.
A man who knows death by heart
Is the man for that life.
In pleasant peace and security
How suddenly the soul in a man begins to die.
He shall look up above the stalled oxen
Envying the cruel falcon,
And dig under the straw for a stone
To bruise himself on.

Love the Wild Swan

This sonnet should be compared with Avison's "Butterfly Bones"
(p. 167). Jeffers' love of the power and reality of the natural world
results, for him, in hatred of the inadequate human world of
art and eventually in self-hatred. Note the echo of Tennyson's
"Lady of Shalott," in which the intrusion of the real
world also cracks the mirror of art.

"I hate my verses, every line, every word.
Oh pale and brittle pencils ever to try
One grass-blade's curve, or the throat of one bird
That clings to twig, ruffled against white sky.
Oh cracked and twilight mirrors ever to catch
One color, one glinting flash, of the splendor of things.
Unlucky hunter, Oh bullets of wax,
The lion beauty, the wild-swan wings, the storm of the wings."
—This wild swan of a world is no hunter's game.
Better bullets than yours would miss the white breast,
Better mirrors than yours would crack in the flame.
Does it matter whether you hate your . . . self? At least
Love your eyes that can see, your mind that can
Hear the music, the thunder of the wings. Love the wild swan.

John Crowe Ransom (1888–   )

Piazza Piece

A clever treatment in dramatic, dialogue form, of the old
theme of death and the lady.

—I am a gentleman in a dustcoat trying
To make you hear. Your ears are soft and small

And listen to an old man not at all,
They want the young men's whispering and sighing.
But see the roses on your trellis dying
And hear the spectral singing of the moon;
For I must have my lovely lady soon,
I am a gentleman in a dustcoat trying.

—I am a lady young in beauty waiting
Until my truelove comes, and then we kiss.
But what grey man among the vines is this
Whose words are dry and faint as in a dream?
Back from my trellis, Sir, before I scream!
I am a lady young in beauty waiting.

The Tall Girl

*Effective contrast between an allegorical theme and the vividly
realistic means the poet employs to dramatize it. The formal, suave
tone and diction of the Queens of Hell contrasts with the
informal and tart tone of the Queen of Heaven, commenting in
a fresh and lively way on the deceptive delights of the primrose
path versus the straight and narrow way.*

The Queens of Hell had lissome necks to crane
At the tall girl approaching with long tread
And, when she was caught up even with them, nodded:
"If the young miss with gold hair might not disdain,
We would esteem her company over the plain,
To profit us all where the dogs will be out barking;
And we'll walk by the windows where the young men are
    working
And to-morrow we will all come home again."

But the Queen of Heaven on the other side of the road
In the likeness, I hear, of a fine motherly woman
Made a wry face, despite it was so common
To be worsted by the smooth ladies of hell,
And crisped her sweet tongue: "This never will come to good!
Just an old woman, my pet, that wishes you well."

Conrad Aiken (1889–)

"Green, green, and green again . . ."

*Structure and movement combine in a beautiful modern treatment
of a traditional theme. Surging onward like the seasons with its
repetition in word and phrase, each quatrain widens the perspective
from the particular geographical—*northward*—in the first, to the
whole world—*this kingdom*—in the second, to the cosmos—*greenest
heaven*—in the third. The final couplet links human emotion and
art to the world of nature, yet at the same time contrasts and
separates the human experience from the flux of natural processes.*

Green, green, and green again, and greener still,
spring towards summer bends the immortal bow,
and northward breaks the wave of daffodil,
and northward breaks the wave of summer's snow:
green, green, and green again, and greener yet,
wide as this forest is, which counts its leaves,
wide as this kingdom, in a green sea set,
which round its shores perpetual blossom weaves—
green, green, and green again, and green once more,
the season finds its term—then greenest, even,
when frost at twilight on the leaf lies hoar,
and one cold star shines bright in greenest heaven:
but love, like music, keeps no seasons ever;
like music, too, once known is known forever.

"Shape has no shape . . ."

Shape has no shape, nor will your thinking shape it,
space has no confines, and no borders time;

and yet, to think the abyss is to escape it,
or fix that horror's margin in a rhyme;
wind blows from heaven, the worlds from chaos pour,
pour into chaos, gone again; the night
foams on an emptiness that has no shore;
and all infinity like leaves in flight—
all flowing, passing, like the bloodstream, here,
that shapes its whispered moment in your hand,
shapes too the hand that holds this moment dear,
itself already pouring into sand;
yet, in the instant that we think it, will
that chaos shape our kiss, and so be still.

Archibald MacLeish (1892–   )

The End of the World

*Particularly effective in its contrast: concrete, detailed, organized
confusion in the octave is set against vast, generalized, abstract
nothingness in the sestet. MacLeish here uses repetition for a
crescendo effect that builds and increases constantly to the almost
intolerable intensity of the last line.*

Quite unexpectedly as Vasserot
The armless ambidextrian was lighting
A match between his great and second toe
And Ralph the lion was engaged in biting
The neck of Madame Sossman while the drum
Pointed, and Teeny was about to cough
In waltz-time swinging Jocko by the thumb—
Quite unexpectedly the top blew off:

And there, there overhead, there, there, hung over
Those thousands of white faces, those dazed eyes,
There in the starless dark the poise, the hover,

There with vast wings across the canceled skies,
There in the sudden blackness the black pall
Of nothing, nothing, nothing—nothing at all.

Wilfred Owen (1893–1918)

Anthem for Doomed Youth

*Through contrasts the poet suggests the negation of ordinary
traditional values by war. The bells, prayers, and songs of Christian
death are parodied by the guns and shells; the candles, funeral
palls, and flowers of dead soldiers are to be found only in the grief
of those bereaved by their deaths. The power of the poem lies in the
justness and aptness of its images and in its strong suggestion that
customary religious rituals and symbols would now be mockery
for the deaths of these "who die as cattle." Religion and its
traditional values have become impotent and meaningless
in the face of modern war.*

What passing-bells for these who die as cattle?
  Only the monstrous anger of the guns.
  Only the stuttering rifles' rapid rattle
Can patter out their hasty orisons.
No mockeries now for them; no prayers nor bells,
  Nor any voice of mourning save the choirs,—
The shrill, demented choirs of wailing shells;
  And bugles calling for them from sad shires.

What candles may be held to speed them all?
  Not in the hands of boys, but in their eyes
Shall shine the holy glimmers of good-byes.
  The pallor of girls' brows shall be their pall;
Their flowers the tenderness of patient minds,
And each slow dusk a drawing-down of blinds.

The End

Notable for its image of the Last Judgment in military terms, for its rhetorical grandeur, and for its grave refusal of spiritual hope and comfort. Owen wrote realistic war poetry, for the most part, but his most successful war poems, like this sonnet, put the particular experience of war into a larger, more universal context.

After the blast of lightning from the east,
The flourish of loud clouds, the Chariot Throne;
After the drums of time have rolled and ceased,
And by the bronze west long retreat is blown,

Shall Life renew these bodies? Of a truth
All death will he annul, all tears assuage?—
Or fill these void veins full again with youth,
And wash, with an immortal water, Age?

When I do ask white Age he saith not so:
"My head hangs weighed with snow."
And when I hearken to the Earth, she saith:
"My fiery heart shrinks, aching. It is death.
Mine ancient scars shall not be glorified,
Nor my titanic tears, the seas, be dried."

Winifred Welles (1893–1939)

Cruciform

Here in the sand, where someone laid him down,
The one known human signature is clear.
Whether woman or man, white-skinned or brown,
Whether the outflung arms were so for fear,

Or agony, or weariness, or shame,
Here, in one line athwart another line,
Is briefly written the one mutual name,
A savior's, or a thief's, or yours, or mine.
Dunes sifted undersea long since have borne
This selfsame cross, small and anonymous.
Tan deserts that the wind has not yet worn
Will print this symbol, and not one of us
But then, or some day, could lie down and fit
Our desolate arms and bodies into it.

Edna St. Vincent Millay (1892–1950)

"See where Capella with her golden kids"

See where Capella with her golden kids
Grazes the slope between the east and north:
Thus when the builders of the pyramids
Flung down their tools at nightfall and poured forth
Homeward to supper and a poor man's bed,
Shortening the road with friendly jest and slur,
The risen She-Goat showing blue and red
Climbed the clear dusk, and three stars followed her.
Safe in their linen and their spices lie
The kings of Egypt; even as long ago
Under these constellations, with long eye
And scented limbs they slept, and feared no foe.
Their will was law; their will was not to die:
And so they had their way; or nearly so.

On Hearing a Symphony of Beethoven

Sweet sounds, oh, beautiful music, do not cease!
Reject me not into the world again.
With you alone is excellence and peace,

Mankind made plausible, his purpose plain.
Enchanted in your air benign and shrewd,
With limbs a-sprawl and empty faces pale,
The spiteful and the stingy and the rude
Sleep like the scullions in the fairy-tale.
This moment is the best the world can give:
The tranquil blossom on the tortured stem.
Reject me not, sweet sounds! oh, let me live,
Till Doom espy my towers and scatter them,
A city spell-bound under the aging sun,
Music my rampart, and my only one.

"I shall forget you presently, my dear"

I shall forget you presently, my dear,
So make the most of this, your little day,
Your little month, your little half a year,
Ere I forget, or die, or move away,
And we are done forever; by and by
I shall forget you, as I said, but now,
If you entreat me with your loveliest lie
I will protest you with my favourite vow.
I would indeed that love were longer-lived,
And oaths were not so brittle as they are,
But so it is, and nature has contrived
To struggle on without a break thus far,—
Whether or not we find what we are seeking
Is idle, biologically speaking.

E. E. Cummings (1894–1962)

1–"the Cambridge ladies . . ."

*Much like Eliot's early poetry. Comments on the emptiness of
modern life are obvious. Both intellect and natural sensibility are*

*voids—the individual and the universe are treated in like manner
—sterile, vapid, meaningless. Succinct diction is the key to the
poem in the description of minds as simultaneously "unbeautiful"
and "comfortable." Christ and Longfellow considered alike by the
ladies presents an ironic contrast understood in the context of
furnished souls. At first the scheme seems unconventional;
however, the octave and sestet are made particularly obvious in
the rhyming of lines 1 and 8, 9 and 14. Cummings also uses
the five-stress line throughout.*

the Cambridge ladies who live in furnished souls
are unbeautiful and have comfortable minds
(also, with the church's protestant blessings
daughters, unscented shapeless spirited)
they believe in Christ and Longfellow, both dead,
are invariably interested in so many things—
at the present writing one still finds
delighted fingers knitting for the is it Poles?
perhaps. While permanent faces coyly bandy
scandal of Mrs. N and Professor D
. . . . the Cambridge ladies do not care, above
Cambridge if sometimes in its box of
sky lavender and cornerless, the
moon rattles like a fragment of angry candy

3–"next to of course god . . ."

*A satiric sonnet on patriotism and war. The voice is that of an
orator speaking on a patriotic occasion. Certainly a useful
comparison is possible with the sonnets of Owen, Blunden, and
Babcock. Here Cummings compresses the images of song and glory
so prevalent during war into images of horror and helplessness—
there is no ring in death—deaf, dumb, mute. The understatement
of the final line after the speaker finishes is an ironic comment on
patriotic speeches in general; they, too, are over soon and hardly
heard. He spoke slows the pace of the poem, which to this point
has been in the jaunty rhythm of marches and patriotic hymns. The
pause allows the reader time to reflect on the satire which has*

preceded. The use of rapidly *in the last line emphasizes the orator's own disbelief in the patriotism he asserts.*

> "next to of course god america i
> love you land of the pilgrims' and so forth oh
> say can you see by the dawn's early my
> country 'tis of centuries come and go
> and are no more what of it we should worry
> in every language even deafanddumb
> thy sons acclaim your glorious name by gorry
> by jingo by gee by gosh by gum
> why talk of beauty what could be more beaut-
> iful than these heroic happy dead
> who rushed like lions to the roaring slaughter
> they did not stop to think they died instead
> then shall the voice of liberty be mute?"
>
> He spoke. And drank rapidly a glass of water

4-"this is the garden . . ."

Rare for Cummings is this sonnet in strict rhyme and meter. The theme is romantic, full of nostalgia, innocence, and dreams. Pastoral in its tone and imagery, the poem is reminiscent of Keats and Shelley. Certainly the Garden of Eden with the figures of Adam and Eve presented in bas-relief is idyllic—captured in one moment for all time.

> this is the garden: colours come and go,
> frail azures fluttering from night's outer wing
> strong silent greens serenely lingering,
> absolute lights like baths of golden snow.
> This is the garden: pursed lips do blow
> upon cool flutes within wide glooms, and sing
> (of harps celestial to the quivering string)
> invisible faces hauntingly and slow.

This is the garden. Time shall surely reap
and on Death's blade lie many a flower curled,
in other lands where other songs be sung;
yet stand They here enraptured, as among
the slow deep trees perpetual of sleep
some silver-fingered fountain steals the world.

5–"if i have made,my lady . . ."

*Cummings here works in a romantic mode—he addresses the lady
he idealizes. Note the only commas in the poem are for the ap-
positive "my lady." Alliteration is particularly effective throughout: the s sound dominates. The rhymes have romantic connota-
tions: snare/hair, stole/soul, wrong/song, slips/lips, came/shame.
Traditional, too, is the octave that presents the dramatic situation,
and the sestet that provides the resolution. The last two lines
present a typically romantic image: "the sweet small clumsy feet
of April came/into the ragged meadow of my soul."*

if i have made,my lady,intricate
imperfect various things chiefly which wrong
your eyes(frailer than most deep dreams are frail)
songs less firm than your body's whitest song
upon my mind—if i have failed to snare
the glance too shy—if through my singing slips
the very skillful strangeness of your smile
the keen primeval silence of your hair

—let the world say "his most wise music stole
nothing from death"—
                          you only will create
(who are so perfectly alive)my shame:
lady through whose profound and fragile lips
the sweet small clumsy feet of April came

into the ragged meadow of my soul.

14–"pity this busy monster . . ."

Cummings, the satirist, in this poem turns his attention to man and the world he has created. The medical, scientific metaphor is unmistakably twentieth-century. The speaker is a physician who describes man and his disease—progress—as beyond both life and death. The world, also identified as the disease, is made, not born; the deity is science exaggerated beyond known limits by the vocabulary Cummings creates: hypermagical, ultraomnipotent. *The entire poem turns on contrast:* pity/not, bigness/littleness, manunkind, born/made, unself, unwish. *There is also the perfection of the satiric tone in the last three lines: the disease is fatal, so let's get the Hell out of here.*

pity this busy monster,manunkind,

not. Progress is a comfortable disease:
your victim(death and life safely beyond)

plays with the bigness of his littleness
—electrons deify one razorblade
into a mountainrange;lenses extend

unwish through curving wherewhen till unwish
returns on its unself.
                        A world of made
is not a world of born—pity poor flesh

and trees,poor stars and stones,but never this
fine specimen of hypermagical

ultraomnipotence. We doctors know

a hopeless case if—listen:there's a hell
of a good universe next door;let's go

24–"i like my body . . ."

Sensual, personal, dramatic rendering of sexual love and fulfill-
ment. The repetition of the verb like *constantly reinforces the*
sense of completion and ecstasy that occurs each time the man and
woman in the poem enjoy sexual love. The total experience of
sex and love, physical and spiritual, is the essence of this sonnet.

i like my body when it is with your
body. It is so quite new a thing.
Muscles better and nerves more.
i like your body. i like what it does,
i like its hows. i like to feel the spine
of your body and its bones, and the trembling
-firm-smooth ness and which i will
again and again and again
kiss, i like kissing this and that of you,
i like, slowly stroking the, shocking fuzz
of your electric fur, and what-is-it comes
over parting flesh. . . . And eyes big love-crumbs,

and possibly i like the thrill
of under me you so quite new

28–"serene immediate silliest . . ."

Cummings' diction depicts, satirically, the mechanical, automatic
woman Hollywood has created. She is a toy within the "Toy,"
controlled, moving like a marionette, though there is no human
nor humane force involved; she is "packed" and "released." There
is an implied comparison between the modern artificial woman
produced by a synthetic culture and the women of Venice in
Browning's poem "A Toccata of Galuppi's," particularly in the
repetition of the phrase "and such hair." Browning tells us that
"mirth and folly were the crop" in Venice; Cummings shows us
the silliness of our own "vicarious ughhuh world."

serene immediate silliest and whose
vast one function being to enter a Toy and
emerging(believably enlarged)make how
many stopped millions of female hard for their
millions of stopped male to look at(now
-fed infantile eyes drooling unmind
grim yessing childflesh perpetually acruise
and her quick way of slowly staring and such hair)
the Californian handpicked thrill mechanically
packed and released for all this very diminishing
vicarious ughhuh world(the pertly papped
muchmouthed)her way of beginningly finishing
(and such hair) the expensively democratic tyrannically dumb

Awake,chaos:we have napped.

"honour corruption villainy holiness"

*Compare this celebration of Chaucer with Wordsworth's "London,
1802" (p. 74). The difference between the Shakespearean and the
Italian form is obvious; but the differences in rhyme (which here
are half-rhymes), syntax, and diction are more important. The latter
are modern; that is, words turn upon themselves—adverbs become
nouns, nouns become adverbs. It is these words that create the
intensely dramatic movement and meaning of the pilgrims who
come to life in the sonnet.*

honour corruption villainy holiness
riding in fragrance of sunlight(side by side
all in a singing wonder of blossoming yes
riding)to him who died that death should be dead

humblest and proudest eagerly wandering
(equally all alive in miraculous day)
merrily moving through sweet forgiveness of spring
(over the under the gift of the earth of the sky

knight and ploughman pardoner wife and nun
merchant frere clerk somnour miller and reve

and geoffrey and all)come up from the never of when
come into the now of forever come riding alive

down while crylessly drifting through vast most
nothing's own nothing children go of dust

Edmund Blunden (1896–   )

Vlamertinghe: Passing the Chateau, July 1917

*Blunden, who served with the British forces through World War I,
here uses a great romantic poem, Keats' "Ode On a Grecian Urn,"
to imply ironically the failure of tradition. The sonnet deftly quotes
—"And all her silken flanks with garlands drest"—parodies—
"Spite of those brute guns lowing at the skies"—mocks Keatsian
diction—"Such damask! such vermillion!"—and in its last two lines
quietly but savagely suggests that, in the modern world, Keats'
famous dictum "Beauty is truth, truth beauty" is quite literally
a bloody falsehood: the red of the poppies in Flanders' fields is
aesthetically false, for it is too bright to camouflage effectively
the duller crimson of blood.*

'And all her silken flanks with garlands drest'—
But we are coming to the sacrifice.
Must those have flowers who are not yet gone West?
May those have flowers who live with death and lice?
This must be the floweriest place
That earth allows; the queenly face
Of the proud mansion borrows grace for grace
Spite of those brute guns lowing at the skies.

Bold great daisies, golden lights,
Bubbling roses' pinks and whites—
Such a gay carpet! poppies by the million;
Such damask! such vermillion!

But if you ask me, mate, the choice of colour
Is scarcely right; this red should have been much duller.

Allan Tate (*1899–*   )

Sonnets at Christmas: II

Poem of personal reminiscence and self-knowledge. There is an
echo of Tennyson's longing, and the Victorian attitude toward
faith. Past and present merge. Christ knows all and judges
according to that knowledge. Contrast the attitude towards sin in
this poem with that of Jeffers, Aiken, or Kunitz.

Ah, Christ, I love you rings to the wild sky
And I must think a little of the past:
When I was ten I told a stinking lie
That got a black boy whipped; but now at last
The going years, with an accurate glow,
Reverse like balls englished upon green baize—
Let them return, let the round trumpets blow
The ancient crackle of the Christ's deep gaze.
Deafened and blind, with senses yet unfound,
Am I, untutored to the after-wit
Of knowledge, knowing a nightmare has no sound;
Therefore with idle hands and head I sit
In late December before the fire's daze
Punished by crimes of which I would be quit.

Leonie Adams (1899–   )

Thought's End

I'd watched the hills drink the last colour of light,
All shapes grow bright and wane on the pale air,
Till down the traitorous east there came the night
And swept the circle of my seeing bare;
Its intimate beauty like a wanton's veil
Tore from the void as from an empty face.
I felt at being's rim all being fail,
And my one body pitted against space.
O heart more frightened than a wild bird's wings
Beating at green, now is no fiery mark
Left on the quiet nothingness of things.
Be self no more against the flooding dark;
There thousandwise, sown in that cloudy blot,
Stars that are worlds look out and see you not.

Yvor Winters (1900–   )

To Emily Dickinson

*There is a pastoral and lyric quality in Winters' poem to Dickinson.
The juxtaposition of the speaker's pilgrimage with that of the one
spoken to is achieved through connectives in the octave: If, Then,
and the shift from I to You in the sestet. The sonnet is itself a
pilgrimage from poetry to God: "Dear Emily, my tears would
burn your page,/. . . In that hard argument which led to God."*

Dear Emily, my tears would burn your page,
But for the fire-dry line that makes them burn—
Burning my eyes, my fingers, while I turn
Singly the words that crease my heart with age.
If I could make some tortured pilgrimage
Through words or Time or the blank pain of Doom
And kneel before you as you found your tomb,
Then I might rise to face my heritage.

Yours was an empty upland solitude
Bleached to the powder of a dying name;
The mind, lost in a word's lost certitude
That faded as the fading footsteps came
To trace an epilogue to words grown odd
In that hard argument which led to God.

Roy Campbell (1901–   )

The Serf

*A fine example of the sonnet's capacity for firm but unobtrusive
balance, parallelism, and antithesis in its structure and of its
relation of the particular to the universal. The serf here, pictured
by a South African poet, is the descendant of Zulu warriors, now
fallen from their military prowess and glory. "But," as the sonnet
turns in the ninth line, he becomes a symbol of the enduring
virtues and values of creation and fruition rather than destruction.*

His naked skin clothed in the torrid mist
That puffs in smoke around the patient hooves,
The ploughman drives, a slow somnambulist,
And through the green his crimson furrow grooves.
His heart, more deeply than he wounds the plain,
Long by the rasping share of insult torn,
Red clod, to which the war-cry once was rain

And tribal spears the fatal sheaves of corn,
Lies fallow now. But as the turf divides
I see in the slow progress of his strides
Over the toppled clods and falling flowers,
The timeless, surly patience of the serf
That moves the nearest to the naked earth
And ploughs down palaces, and thrones, and towers.

Familiar Daemon

*Here Campbell unites romantic and modern in echoes of Eliot's
"The Lovesong of J. Alfred Prufrock" and Keats' "Ode to the
Nightingale." The imagery is of the imagination—flagons/dragons.
The "hellward rider" is imagination. Tetrameter lines and octo-
syllables hark back to the ballads. Thus the poem achieves a gothic
quality. Cripple refers to most of mankind—those unable to enjoy
imagination, and who, without it, cannot be whole. Even the
threat of death cannot separate the poet from the spirit and
inspiration of imagination.*

Measuring out my life in flagons
(No coffee-spoon to skim the flood)
You were the prince of thirsty dragons,
The gay carouser of my blood:
We could not part, our love was such,
But gasconading, shared the fun
While every cripple's shouldered crutch
Was sighted at me like a gun.
What sport today? to swim or fly,
Or fish for thunder in the sky?
What laughter out of hell to fetch,
Or joy from peril, have you planned,
You hellward rider, that you stretch
The downswung stirrup of my hand?

Merrill Moore (1903–1957)

How She Resolved to Act

"I shall be careful to say nothing at all
About myself or what I know of him
Or the vaguest thought I have—no matter how dim,
Tonight if it so happen that he call."

And not ten minutes later the door-bell rang
And into the hall he stepped as he always did
With a face and a bearing that quite poorly hid
His brain that burned and his heart that fairly sang
And his tongue that wanted to be rid of the truth.

As well as she could, for she was very loath
To signify how she felt, she kept very still,
But soon her heart cracked loud as a coffee mill
And her brain swung like a comet in the dark
And her tongue raced like a squirrel in the park.

Stanley Kunitz (1905–   )

Organic Bloom

Another sonnet in strict traditional form. Emphasis, however, is twentieth-century, and the theme is nihilistic. The diction is contemporary; the metaphor scientific, even medical. The self is responsible for its own limitations; and from its own construct, it spreads destruction. Tone and voice are gloomy.

The brain constructs its systems to enclose
The steady paradox of thought and sense;
Momentously its tissued meaning grows
To solve and integrate experience.
But life escapes closed reason. We explain
Our chaos into cosmos, cell by cell,
Only to learn of some insidious pain
Beyond the limits of our charted hell,
A guilt not mentioned in our prayers, a sin
Conceived against the self. So, vast and vaster
The plasmic circles of gray discipline
Spread outward to include each new disaster.
Enormous floats the brain's organic bloom
Till, bursting like a fruit, it scatters doom.

Rex Warner (1905–   )

Mallard

*Compare this sonnet with Clare's "Signs of Winter" (p. 83).
Contemporary in diction and image, far less rigid in structure and
movement, the modern sonnet has the same unpretentious realism,
the same genre painter's eye for detail as the earlier poem.*

Squawking they rise from reeds into the sun,
climbing like furies, running on blood and bone,
with wings like garden shears clipping the misty air,
four mallard, hard winged, with necks like rods
fly in perfect formation over the marsh.

Keeping their distance, gyring, not letting slip the air,
but leaping into it straight like hounds or divers,
they stretch out into the wind and sound their horns again.

Suddenly siding to a bank of air unbidden
by hand signal or morse message of command
downsky they plane, sliding like corks on a current,
designed so deftly that all air is advantage,

till, with few flaps, orderly as they left earth,
alighting among curlew they pad on mud.

W. H. Auden (1907–   )

Our Bias

*A modern, light-handed treatment of an old theme: the alienation
and separation of man from nature. The worlds of instinct and
reason, concretion and abstraction, simplicity and complexity,
action and contemplation, are contrasted in the symbols of the
octave; and the sestet comments on human nature and its per-
versity with wry, ironic humor.*

The hour-glass whispers to the lion's paw,
The clock-towers tell the gardens day and night,
How many errors Time has patience for,
How wrong they are in being always right.

Yet Time, however loud its chimes or deep,
However fast its falling torrent flows,
Has never put the lion off his leap
Nor shaken the assurance of the rose.

For they, it seems, care only for success:
While we choose words according to their sound
And judge a problem by its awkwardness;

And Time with us was always popular.
When have we not preferred some going round
To going straight to where we are?

Sonnets from China: XII

Another treatment, in the context of war, of a favorite modern theme: the contrast between living realities and the power of abstractions. Compare this poem with Avison's "Butterfly Bones" (p. 167). The theme is a prominent one in the fiction of this century as well as in poetry.

Here war is harmless like a monument:
A telephone is talking to a man;
Flags on a map declare that troops were sent;
A boy brings milk in bowls. There is a plan

For living men in terror of their lives,
Who thirst at nine who were to thirst at noon,
Who can be lost and are, who miss their wives
And, unlike an idea, can die too soon.

Yet ideas can be true, although men die:
For we have seen a myriad faces
Ecstatic from one lie,

And maps can really point to places
Where life is evil now.
Nanking. Dachau.

A Voyage: III

A modern answer to the ancient "riddle of the Sphinx." The poet takes the Sphinx itself as a symbol of the pain and meaninglessness of the world.

Did it once issue from the carver's hand
Healthy? Even the earliest conqueror saw
The face of a sick ape, a bandaged paw,
An ailing lion crouched on dirty sand.

We gape, then go uneasily away:
It does not like the young nor love nor learning.
Time hurt it like a person: it lies turning
A vast behind on shrill America,

And witnesses. The huge hurt face accuses
And pardons nothing, least of all success:
What counsel it might offer it refuses
To those who face akimbo its distress.

'Do people like me?' *No.* The slave amuses
The lion. 'Am I to suffer always?' *Yes.*

The Novelist

Encased in talent like a uniform,
The rank of every poet is well known;
They can amaze us like a thunderstorm,
Or die so young, or live for years alone.

They can dash forward like hussars: but he
Must struggle out of his boyish gift and learn
How to be plain and awkward, how to be
One after whom none think it worth to turn.

For, to achieve his lightest wish, he must
Become the whole of boredom, subject to
Vulgar complaints like love, among the Just

Be just, among the Filthy filthy too,
And in his own weak person, if he can,
Must suffer dully all the wrongs of Man.

Stephen Spender (1909–   )

Daybreak

*A beautiful and successful melding of the traditional and modern.
The irregular stresses, half rhymes, and intimate personal tone
set off and emphasize the highly romantic diction, subject, and
attitude. This poem makes an instructive comparison and contrast
with Rossetti's "Nuptial Sleep" (p. 118), in any attempt to define
what romantic means in different periods.*

At dawn she lay with her profile at that angle
Which, sleeping, seems the stone face of an angel;
Her hair a harp the hand of a breeze follows
To play, against the white cloud of the pillows.
Then in a flush of rose she woke, and her eyes were open
Swimming with blue through the rose flesh of dawn.
From her dew of lips, the drop of one word
Fell, from a dawn of fountains, when she murmured
"Darling," upon my heart the song of the first bird.
"My dream glides in my dream," she said, "come true.
I waken from you to my dream of you."
O then my waking dream dared to assume
The audacity of her sleep. Our dreams
Flowed into each other's arms, like streams.

Christopher Hassall (*1912–*)

Crisis: No. XXVII

Compare with earlier war poems, like Blunden's (p. 201) and Owen's (pp. 191 and 192) for both similarity and contrast. There is, it must be admitted, a touch of contrivance here in both images and dialogue; but it is successful contrivance, for both image and dialogue make a powerful effect.

Look at the searchlights! There's a fire in heaven,
And we have turned our hoses on the sky.
Look at that flock of birds, daring to fly
Across the luminous torrent, never driven
To earth, but coming thickly on in tens,
Twenties and hundreds, silvering overhead.
—Your dare-all birds are aeroplanes, I said,
Whose passengers are heavy fountain-pens.
—What will they write?
              Death-warrants.
                   Who must die?
Since you demand an answer: You and I.
My friend grew pale. Is this our Judgement-Day?
How have we sinned? How have these Things intruded
On our sweet sleep? Who made them, anyway?
Startled, we both replied together—You Did.

John Gawsworth (1912–   )

Edward Thomas

Compare this sonnet of elegy to Gray's "On the Death of Mr. Richard West" (p. 63).

When rime was on the road, and ditches glistened
Under the leafless trees before the hedge,
The birds upon the boughs perked heads, and listened
To the tight ice, cracking amid the sedge;
And over the old bridge you came a-whistling,
Puffing your mouth, steaming the air around,
And I thought: 'Never the scytheman went a-thistling
That cut his purple clean as you cut sound.'

Your notes re-echo on a frosty morning:
I never see the sun's bar top a hill,
The ice-plumed pine with dripping fire adorning,
But once again I hear their lusty, shrill,
Clear music, and expect to see you come,
I cannot think: 'He's turned and made for home.'

Dylan Thomas (1914–1953)

On the Marriage of a Virgin

Thomas does break away from conventional rhyme, meter, and division. The rhymes are often half-rhymes, the stresses range from four to eight, and the division is two septets. Imagery is a mixture of sensual and religious. Christ and the miracle of feeding the multitude and the image of the Holy Ghost reflect the glory of marriage as sacrament. Note the use of diction to equate the sensual and religious: multitude of loves/miraculous . . . loaves.

Waking alone in a multitude of loves when morning's light
Surprised in the opening of her nightlong eyes
His golden yesterday asleep upon the iris
And this day's sun leapt up the sky out of her thighs
Was miraculous virginity old as loaves and fishes,
Though the moment of a miracle is unending lightning
And the shipyards of Galilee's footprints hide a navy of doves.

No longer will the vibrations of the sun desire on
Her deepsea pillow where once she married alone,
Her heart all ears and eyes, lips catching the avalanche
Of the golden ghost who ringed with his streams her mercury
   bone,
Who under the lids of her windows hoisted his golden luggage,
For a man sleeps where fire leapt down and she learns through
   his arm
That other sun, the jealous coursing of the unrivalled blood.

Among Those Killed in a Dawn Raid Was a Man Aged a Hundred

A sonnet on the uselessness and waste of war, its inhumanity and depersonalization. Again, not the traditional divisions; the sonnet is in four parts. Lines 1–5 describe the dramatic setting, lines 6–9 compare the aged man to the unlocked doors around him in keys and chains; lines 10–11 lock again with the cage image; lines 12–14 plead for recognition and assume a rebirth in a hundred storks. Compare with the poems of Owen and Hassall.

When the morning was waking over the war
He put on his clothes and stepped out and he died,
The locks yawned loose and a blast blew them wide,
He dropped where he loved on the burst pavement stone

And the funeral grains of the slaughtered floor.
Tell his street on its back he stopped a sun
And the craters of his eyes grew springshoots and fire
When all the keys shot from the locks, and rang.
Dig no more for the chains of his grey-haired heart.
The heavenly ambulance drawn by a wound
Assembling waits for the spade's ring on the cage.
O keep his bones away from that common cart,
The morning is flying on the wings of his age
And a hundred storks perch on the sun's right hand.

John Berryman (1914–1972)

Not to Live

A fascinating, commemorative sonnet on the three hundred fiftieth anniversary of the founding of Jamestown. Irregular stresses and enjambement give the poem an abrupt, frightened tone. Note all of the words that connote indecision and the modern diction that describes an event many years old.

It kissed us, soft, to cut our throats, this coast,
like a malice of the lazy King. I hunt,
& hunt! but find here what to kill?—nothing is blunt,
but phantoming uneases I find. Ghost
on ghost precedes of all most scared us, most
we fled. Howls fail upon this secret, far air: grunt,
shaming for food; you must. I love the King
& it was not I who strangled at the toast
but a flux of a free & dying adjutant:
God be with him. He & God be with us all,
for we are not to live. I cannot wring,
like laundry, blue my soul—indecisive thing . . .
From undergrowth & over odd birds call
and who would starv'd so survive? God save the King.

John Manifold (1915–   )

The Sirens

Compare with Lang's "The Odyssey" (p. 137) to see how the modern poet uses the past to comment on the present in a new way. No longer does the poet turn to the great literature of the past as a refuge. Odysseus here is modern man himself in the midst of crisis. The siren voices of all traditional sources of value —art, nature, sex, science and industry, society itself—are forgotten in the need to cope with the bloody serious situation. Note how deftly and with what humorous effect Manifold combines contemporary and traditional symbols.

Odysseus heard the sirens; they were singing
Music by Wolf and Weinberger and Morley
About a region where the swans go winging,
Vines are in colour, girls are growing surely

Into nubility, and pylons bringing
Leisure and power to farms that live securely
Without a landlord. Still, his eyes were stinging
With salt and sea blink, and the ropes hurt sorely.

Odysseus saw the sirens; they were charming,
Blonde, with snub breasts and little neat posteriors,
But could not take his mind off the alarming

Weather report, his mutineers in irons,
The radio failing; it was bloody serious.
In twenty minutes he forgot the sirens.

Robert Lowell (1917–   )

Words for Hart Crane

A fine, condensed biography of the tragic life of an earlier Ameri-
can poet and a contemporary treatment of the conflict of the artist
with society—a theme that became prominent in the later nineteenth
century. Note how dramatically Lowell presents his commentary on
Crane's poetry and plight.

> "When the Pulitzers showered on some dope
> or screw who flushed our dry mouths out with soap,
> few people would consider why I took
> to stalking sailors, and scattered Uncle Sam's
> phoney gold-plated laurels to the birds.
> Because I knew my Whitman like a book,
> stranger in America, tell my country: I,
> *Catullus redivivus,* once the rage
> of the Village and Paris, used to play my role
> of homosexual, wolfing the stray lambs
> who hungered by the Place de la Concorde.
> My profit was a pocket with a hole.
> Who asks for me, the Shelley of my age,
> must lay his heart out for my bed and board."

Concord

The conventional Italian sonnet in an enormously successful accom-
modation to contemporary theme, diction, and image. Note Lowell's
word play and puns, and particularly his ironic use of earlier
literature. Emerson's "rude bridge that arched the flood" is "ruined"
here; Thoreau's classic account of an earlier retreat from the modern
world is recalled in Walden's fished-out perch; the Unitarian Church

"rings out" Jesus in a sense far different from that used by Tenny-
son in his lyric "Ring out, wild bells . . ."; as for the announcement
of a new nation, Lowell reminds us that it was conceived not in
liberty but in injustice and brutality. It is the scream of the mur-
dered King Philip that is heard around the world, and its echo
"girdled this imperfect globe" also in the sense in which an injury
to its bark girdles and hence kills a tree. In its fourteen lines this
sonnet offers a view of history, a comment on tradition and faith,
and a trenchant satire on what the present has made of the hopes
and aspirations of the past. "Heraclitus' stream" is, of course, the
river of time. Heraclitus, a Greek philosopher, says "no man can
step into the same river twice."

Ten thousand Fords are idle here in search
Of a tradition. Over these dry sticks—
The Minute Man, the Irish Catholics,
The ruined bridge and Walden's fished-out perch—
The belfry of the Unitarian Church
Rings out the hanging Jesus. Crucifix,
How can your whited spindling arms transfix
Mammon's unbridled industry, the lurch
For forms to harness Heraclitus' stream!
This Church is Concord—Concord where Thoreau
Named all the birds without a gun to probe
Through darkness to the painted man and bow:
The death-dance of King Philip and his scream
Whose echo girdled this imperfect globe.

Elizabeth Jennings (1926–   )

Lazarus

It was the amazing white, it was the way he simply
Refused to answer our questions, it was the cold pale glance
Of death upon him, the smell of death that truly

Declared his rising to us. It was no chance
Happening, as a man may fill a silence
Between two heart-beats, seem to be dead and then
Astonish us with the closeness of his presence;
This man was dead, I say it again and again.
All of our sweating bodies moved towards him
And our minds moved too, hungry for finished faith.
He would not enter our world at once with words
That we might be tempted to twist or argue with:
Cold like a white root pressed in the bowels of earth
He looked but also vulnerable—like birth.

Donald Hall (1928–   )

The Funeral

*Simple in diction and direct in statement. Though concerned with
death and personal loss, the poet delights in playing with words.
Note the pun: "It is the box from which no jack will spring."
Contrast of death and life is particularly poignant because of the
quiet tone and the use of understatement in the sestet. The four
feminine endings in the octave and the repetition of the word* close
provide the finality of the poem.

It is the box from which no jack will spring.
Now close the box, but not until she kisses
The crossed, large hands which she already misses
For their caress, and on his hands the ring.
Now close the box, if we close anything.
She sees the wooden lid, and she dismisses
At least a hundred thoughtful artifices
That would enjoy the tears that they would bring.

The coffin does not matter. It was one
Like many in the row from which she chose it.

Now to be closed in it, he must become
Like all the other dead men, deaf and dumb,
Blank to the small particulars that stun
Her mind all day. Black men, now come and close it.

George Barker (*1913–*   )

To My Mother

*An unusual, touching, and effective use of the sonnet for portrait
and for compliment. Compare with Henley's "Apparition" (p. 152).*

Most near, most dear, most loved and most far,
Under the window where I often found her
Sitting as huge as Asia, seismic with laughter,
Gin and chicken helpless in her Irish hand,
Irresistible at Rabelais, but most tender for
The lame dogs and hurt birds that surround her,—
She is a procession no one can follow after
But be like a little dog following a brass band.

She will not glance up at the bomber, or condescend
To drop her gin and scuttle to a cellar,
But lean on the mahogany table like a mountain
Whom only faith can move, and so I send
O all my faith, and all my love to tell her
That she will move from mourning into morning.

Glossary

Alliteration   the repetition of the same initial sounds in one or more lines of verse

Analogy   a similarity; a partial resemblance between two otherwise dissimilar objects, situations, or ideas

Assonance   the repetition of similar vowel sounds within words

Blank verse   unrhymed iambic pentameter

Caesura   the major pause in a line of poetry, usually in a line containing five or more feet

Conceit   an elaborate or ingenious image; often an extended metaphor or simile that produces a powerful emotional response by means of intellectual manipulation

Consonance   the repetition of similar consonant sounds within words

Convention   a theme or method common to a particular period or literary form. For example, the theme of courtly love in medieval or Renaissance poetry is a *convention,* as is the fourteen-line fixed form of the sonnet.

Couplet   two consecutive, rhyming lines of the same length and meter

Decasyllabic line   a ten-syllable line of verse

Diction   the writer's choice of specific words; his vocabulary and type of language

Ellipsis   omission of a word or words not necessary for understanding, but only for grammatical precision

English sonnet   See *Shakespearean sonnet.*

Enjambment   the running over of the sense and grammatical structure of one line into the next:

> I long have had a quarrel set with Time,
> Because he robbed me. . . .

Epigram   a succinct, often witty saying, often in the form of a closed couplet:

> Thy flattering picture, Phyrne is like thee,
> Only in this, that you both painted be.

Epithet   a two or three word descriptive term applied to an individual

Feminine ending   a line of verse ending on an unstressed syllable, thereby often creating a double rhyme: *seeing/being, frightful/delightful*

Foot   a metrical unit of stressed and unstressed syllables in a particular pattern such as iamb or trochee

Form   the organization of all elements in the poem including both metrics and the arrangement and development of symbolic language

Half-rhyme an imperfect kind of rhyme. Where true rhyme keeps the vowel sound and changes the consonant—*bold/cold*—half-rhyme keeps the consonant sound and changes the vowel—*cold/killed*.

Heroic couplet a rhymed couplet in iambic pentameter

Iamb a two-syllable foot stressed on the second syllable

Image any kind of figurative language such as metaphor, simile, or symbol, illuminating and contributing to the total meaning of the thing described by suggestion rather than logic or literal meaning

Inscape See p. 101 of text.

Italian sonnet See *Petrarchan sonnet.*

Kenning See p. 101 of text.

Masculine ending a line of verse ending on a stressed syllable

Metaphor an implied comparison between two dissimilar objects

Meter the pattern of stressed and unstressed syllables in a line of verse

Mood the total created experience of a poem, including diction, image, tone, sound, and meter; similar to but not synonymous with *tone*

Occasional poetry poems written to commemorate a specific event

Octosyllabic line an eight-syllable line of verse, usually in rhymed couplets

Octave a stanza of eight lines; also the first eight lines of a Petrarchan sonnet

Petrarchan (Italian) sonnet a fourteen-line iambic pentameter poem composed of an octave rhyming *a b b a, a b b a,* and a sestet usually rhyming either *c d c d c d,* or *c d e c d e.* The octave usually presents and develops the theme; the sestet reflects upon or resolves it.

Petrarchismo artificial imitations of the Petrarchan form and conventions. See pp. 5 and 7 of text.

Quatrain a stanza of four lines

Rhyme scheme the pattern of rhymes in a stanza or an entire poem

Sestet a stanza of six lines; also the last six lines of a Petrarchan sonnet

Shakespearean (English) sonnet a fourteen-line iambic pentameter poem composed of three quatrains rhyming *a b a b c d c d e f e f* and a final couplet rhyming *g g.* The quatrains develop the theme; the couplet states a conclusion.

Sonnet sequence a group of sonnets connected by a main theme or themes and written under one title; *e.g.,* Sir Philip Sidney's *Astrophel and Stella* and Dante Gabriel Rossetti's *House of Life.*

Spenserian sonnet Edmund Spenser's variation of the sonnet form in which the poet uses linked rhymes in the quatrains: *a b a b b c b c c d c d e e*

Sprung rhythm See p. 100 of text.

Structure See *Form.*

Symbol a word or image that suggests a meaning and value much larger and more indefinite than its denotative meaning

Syntax the orderly arrangement of words and phrases to show their mutual relationships within a larger grammatical unit such as the sentence

Tercet three lines linked by rhyme

Tetrameter a verse line of four feet

Tone the speaker's attitude toward his subject or situation, conveyed by the poet's choice and management of diction, syntax, image, sound, and meter; similar to but not synonymous with *mood*

Index of Authors

Index of Titles and First Lines